THE CHURCH OF ALL HALLOWS BARKING, BEING THE TWELFTH VOLUME OF THE SURVEY OF LONDON, BY LILIAN J. REDSTONE AND MEMBERS OF THE LONDON SURVEY COMMITTEE

AMS PRESS

NEW YORK

THE SOUTH-EAST PROSPECT OF THE CHURCH OF ALHALLOWS BARKING.

LONDON COUNTY COUNCIL

SURVEY OF LONDON

ISSUED BY THE JOINT PUBLISHING COMMITTEE
REPRESENTING THE LONDON COUNTY COUNCIL
AND THE LONDON SURVEY COMMITTEE

UNDER THE GENERAL EDITORSHIP OF

MONTAGU H. COX (*for the Council*)
PHILIP NORMAN (*for the Survey Committee*)

VOLUME XII

THE PARISH OF ALL HALLOWS BARKING
Part I

PUBLISHED FOR THE LONDON COUNTY COUNCIL BY B. T. BATSFORD, LTD.
94, HIGH HOLBORN, LONDON, W.C.
1929

c

Reprinted from the edition of 1929, London

First AMS edition published in 1971

Manufactured in the United States of America

International Standard Book Number:
Complete Set: 0-404-51650-5
Volume XII: 0-404-51662-9

Library of Congress Catalog Card Number: 74-138273

AMS PRESS INC.
NEW YORK, N.Y.   10003

THE CHURCH OF ALL HALLOWS
BARKING, BEING THE TWELFTH
VOLUME OF THE SURVEY OF
LONDON, BY LILIAN J. REDSTONE
AND MEMBERS OF THE LONDON
SURVEY COMMITTEE

JOINT PUBLISHING COMMITTEE REPRESENTING THE LONDON
COUNTY COUNCIL AND THE LONDON SURVEY COMMITTEE

Chairman

SIR ERNEST MEINERTZHAGEN.

Members appointed by the Council

JOHNSON, W. C.   MacDONNELL, J. H.

KARSLAKE, Lt.-Col. J. B. P.   MEINERTZHAGEN, SIR ERNEST.

Members appointed by the London Survey Committee

GODFREY, WALTER H.   LOVELL, PERCY W.

NORMAN, Dr. PHILIP.

iv

MEMBERS OF THE LONDON SURVEY COMMITTEE DURING THE PERIOD OF THE WORK

THE FORMER PRESIDENTS OF THE COMMITTEE WERE—
THE LATE LORD LEIGHTON, P.R.A.
THE LATE RT. HON. AND RT. REV. DR. CREIGHTON, LORD BISHOP OF LONDON.
THE LATE THE MOST HON. THE MARQUESS CURZON OF KEDLESTON, K.G., G.C.S.I., G.C.I.E.

President

THE RT. HON. THE EARL OF CRAWFORD AND BALCARRES, K.T., P.S.A.

Honorary Members and Subscribers

The Rt. Hon. LORD ABERDARE OF DUFFRYN, D.L.
The Rt. Hon. LORD ALDENHAM, F.S.A.
A. A. ALLEN.
The SOCIETY OF ANTIQUARIES OF LONDON.
WILLIAM SUMNER APPLETON.
The ROYAL INSTITUTE OF BRITISH ARCHITECTS.
The ARCHITECTURAL ASSOCIATION.
C. R. ASHBEE, M.A., F.R.I.B.A.
The ATHENÆUM.
JOHN AVERY, F.C.A., F.S.S.
E. BURRELL BAGGALLAY.
Miss HELEN A. D. BARLOW.
P. A. BAYMAN.
BOYLSTON A. BEAL.
WALTER G. BELL, F.S.A.
The BERMONDSEY PUBLIC LIBRARIES.
The Ven. ARCHDEACON BEVAN, M.A.
HENRY FORBES BIGELOW.
HARRY W. BIRKS.
The BIRMINGHAM CENTRAL LIBRARY.
The BISHOPSGATE INSTITUTE.
A. H. BLAKE, M.A., F.R.Hist.S.
ARTHUR BONNER, F.S.A.
ALFRED C. BOSSOM, F.R.I.B.A.

The BRITISH MUSEUM.
E. W. BROOKS.
A. HERVÉ BROWNING.
The CARNEGIE LIBRARY, PITTSBURGH.
The WORSHIPFUL COMPANY OF CARPENTERS.
Miss A. G. E. CARTHEW.
The CHELSEA PUBLIC LIBRARY.
G. H. CHETTLE.
The CHISWICK PUBLIC LIBRARY.
The CHURCH HOUSE LIBRARY.
Sir CYRIL COBB, K.B.E., M.V.O., M.P.
E. C. COLQUHOUN.
The COLUMBIA UNIVERSITY LIBRARY.
The CONSTITUTIONAL CLUB.
WILLIAM W. CORDINGLEY.
The Most Hon. the MARQUESS OF CREWE, K.G.
W. E. VERNON CROMPTON, F.R.I.B.A.
The CROYDON PUBLIC LIBRARY.
Sir GEORGE DUCKWORTH, C.B., F.S.A.
EUSTACE ERLEBACH.
The Rt. Hon. the EARL FERRERS, F.S.A.
The FULHAM PUBLIC LIBRARY.

Miss AGNES GARRETT.
RICHARD L. GIVEEN.
The GOLDSMITHS' LIBRARY, UNIVERSITY OF LONDON.
LADY GRAY.
Miss I. I. GREAVES.
HUBERT J. GREENWOOD, D.L., J.P.
Miss GERTRUDE GUGGENHEIM.
The GUILDHALL LIBRARY.
EDWIN T. GUNN, A.R.I.B.A.
The HACKNEY PUBLIC LIBRARY.
RICHARD WALDEN HALE.
E. STANLEY HALL, M.A., F.R.I.B.A.
The HAMMERSMITH CENTRAL LIBRARY.
ARTHUR F. HILL.
OSBORN C. HILLS, F.R.I.B.A.
The Rt. Hon. Sir SAMUEL HOARE, Bt., C.M.G., M.P.
J. J. HOLDSWORTH.
Mrs. MAUD HORNE.
E. J. HORNIMAN, J.P.
CONSTANT HUNTINGTON.
Maj. DOUGLAS ILLINGWORTH.
Mrs. ILLINGWORTH ILLINGWORTH.
Miss EDITH F. INDERWICK.
The Rt. Hon. VISCOUNT IVEAGH.

v

T. GORDON JACKSON, F.R.I.B.A.
C. H. JARRETT.
C. H. F. KINDERMAN-WALKER.
JAMES E. KING.
F. A. KONIG.
AUBREY T. LAWRENCE, K.C.
The Hon. LADY LAWRENCE.
G. C. LAWSON.
The LADY LECONFIELD.
H. W. LEWER, F.S.A.
OWEN C. LITTLE.
NATHANIEL LLOYD, O.B.E., F.S.A.
LADY LOCKYER.
The LONDON LIBRARY.
The LONDON AND MIDDLESEX ARCHÆOLOGICAL SOCIETY.
The LONDON SCHOOL OF ECONOMICS.
J. LORT-WILLIAMS, K.C.
GILBERT H. LOVEGROVE, F.R.I.B.A.
The Rt. Hon. MARY, COUNTESS OF LOVELACE.
The Rev. WILLIAM MAC-GREGOR, F.S.A.
The MANCHESTER PUBLIC LIBRARIES.
The MANCHESTER SOCIETY OF ARCHITECTS.
Mrs. JOHN MARKOE.
R. W. MAY.
Miss B. A. MEINERTZHAGEN.

The METROPOLITAN PUBLIC GARDENS ASSOCIATION.
W. MONK, R.E.
G. VAUGHAN MORGAN.
JOHN MURRAY, F.R.I.B.A.
The NEW YORK PUBLIC LIBRARY.
The NEWBERRY LIBRARY, CHICAGO.
SYDNEY J. NEWCOMBE.
J. NEWMAN.
RICHARD NICHOLSON.
R. C. NORMAN.
Mrs. ROBERT NORMAN.
The OXFORD AND CAMBRIDGE CLUB.
F. W. PETERS.
The FREE LIBRARY OF PHILADELPHIA.
DAME JESSIE WILTON PHIPPS, D.B.E., J.P.
H. A. PIEHLER.
F. W. PLATT.
ARNOLD DANVERS POWER.
Lt.-Col. Sir D'ARCY POWER, K.B.E., M.A., F.S.A.
ERNEST PRESTIGE.
Major Sir JOHN PRESTIGE.
F. W. PROCTER.
The PUBLIC RECORD OFFICE.
COLIN E. READER.
The REFORM CLUB.
Mrs. F. W. L. RICHARDSON.
The JOHN RYLANDS LIBRARY, MANCHESTER.

The SHOREDITCH PUBLIC LIBRARY.
SION COLLEGE.
Commander SKINNER, R.N.
Mrs. VERNON SMITH.
W. J. SONGHURST.
The SOUTHWARK PUBLIC LIBRARY.
The STOKE NEWINGTON PUBLIC LIBRARY.
R. T. D. STONEHAM.
R. CLIPSTON STURGIS.
Sir ANDREW T. TAYLOR, F.S.A., J.P.
HAMILTON H. TURNER.
The VICTORIA AND ALBERT MUSEUM.
NOEL P. W. VINER-BRADY, F.S.A.
Mrs. MILTON WALDMAN.
LEWIS HUTH WALTERS.
The LIBRARY OF CONGRESS, WASHINGTON.
The WEST HAM PUBLIC LIBRARY.
The CITY OF WESTMINSTER PUBLIC LIBRARIES.
Mrs. WHARRIE.
Miss M. J. WILDE.
HORACE WILKINSON.
The WOOLWICH PUBLIC LIBRARIES.
H.M. OFFICE OF WORKS.
JOHN E. YERBURY.
KEITH D. YOUNG, F.R.I.B.A.

Active Members

OSWALD BARRON, F.S.A.
W. W. BEGLEY, F.R.Hist.S.
*J. W. BLOE, O.B.E., F.S.A.
W. W. BRAINES, B.A. (Lond.)
A. E. BULLOCK, A.R.I.B.A.
*A. W. CLAPHAM, F.S.A.
*The Rev. E. E. DORLING, F.S.A., M.A.
*J. J. EDMUNDS.

*H. W. FINCHAM, F.S.A.
THOMAS F. FORD, A.R.I.B.A.
*G. GORDON GODFREY.
Mrs. ERNEST GODMAN, A.R.E.
T. FRANK GREEN, F.R.I.B.A.
RICHARD HARRISS.
MAX JUDGE.
*P. K. KIPPS, A.R.I.B.A.

B. R. LEFTWICH, M.B.E., F.R.Hist.S.
ERNEST A. MANN, L.R.I.B.A.
W. McB. MARCHAM.
ELLIS MARSLAND.
E. C. NISBET, L.R.I.B.A.
ROBERT PEARSALL.
E. A. R. RAHBULA, M.C., F.S.A.

Francis W. Reader.

Mill Stephenson, B.A., F.S.A.

*Francis R. Taylor, L.R.I.B.A.

T. O. Thirtle, A.R.I.B.A.

*A. H. Thomas, M.A., F.S.A.

*George Trotman.

R. E. Mortimer Wheeler, M.C., M.A., D.Lit., F.S.A.

*Edward Yates.

*W. Plomer Young.

*Philip Norman, LL.D., F.S.A., *Chairman and Hon. Editor of the Committee.*

*Walter H. Godfrey, F.R.I.B.A., F.S.A., *Hon. Assistant Editor of the Committee.*

*Sir Ernest Meinertzhagen, J.P., *Hon. Treasurer of the Committee.*

A. Grayston Warren, F.C.A., *Hon. Auditor of the Committee.*

*Percy W. Lovell, B.A., A.R.I.B.A., F.S.A., *Secretary of the Committee,* Lancaster House, St. James's, S.W.1.

* Denotes those who have co-operated in the production of the present volume.

CONTENTS

	PAGE
GENERAL TITLE PAGE	i
PREVIOUS VOLUMES OF THE "SURVEY OF LONDON"	ii
SPECIAL TITLE PAGE	iii
MEMBERS OF THE JOINT PUBLISHING COMMITTEE	iv
MEMBERS OF THE LONDON SURVEY COMMITTEE	v
DESCRIPTION OF THE PLATES	xi
HERALDIC ILLUSTRATIONS	xiv
PREFACE	xv

THE SURVEY OF THE CHURCH OF ALL HALLOWS BARKING

I. HISTORY:

1. Foundations	1
2. Barking Abbey and the Church	2
3. Dedication of the Church	3
4. The Church and the City	4
5. Sanctuary	5
6. The Trial of the Templars	6
7. The Church and Chancery	8
8. The Royal Lady Chapel	9
9. Royal Charters of the Chapel	13
10. Suppression of the Royal Chapel	18
11. Medieval Worship in All Hallows	20
12. Chapels and Chantries	27
13. The Great Change	34
14. Parish Government	39
15. Laudian All Hallows	41
16. Puritan All Hallows	43
17. The Explosion and Fire of 1649–50	45
18. The Later Growth of Church and Parish	48

II. RECTORS AND VICARS OF ALL HALLOWS	52
III. ARCHITECTURE	54

APPENDICES:

I. Forty days Indulgence to those who pay Devotions in the Chapel in the   PAGE
Churchyard of Berkyngchirche   –   –   –   –   –   –   –   67

II. Inventory of Church Goods, 1452   –   –   –   –   –   –   –   70

III. Inventory of Church Goods, 1506   –   –   –   –   –   –   –   76

IV. Inventory of Church Goods, 1512   –   –   –   –   –   –   –   78

V. Testament and Will of John Croke –   –   –   –   –   –   –   84

VI. Testament and Will of Robert Tate –   –   –   –   –   –   –   89

BIBLIOGRAPHICAL NOTE   –   –   –   –   –   –   –   –   92

INDEX   –   –   –   –   –   –   –   –   –   –   –   –   93

PLATES, Nos. 1 TO 90.

LIST OF PLATES

Frontispiece –   –   The South-East Prospect of the Church of All Hallows Barking.
From the engraving by R. West and W. H. Toms, 1736.

Illustration before text.   All Hallows Church in 1597, from Haiward and Gascoyne's
Survey of the Liberties of the Tower.

EARLY VIEWS

PLATE

1. Exterior from the South-East, *c.* 1800 –   – From an unsigned water-colour drawing in the Crace Collection.

2. Exterior from the South-East, *c.* 1803 –   – From a pencil drawing by C. J. M. Whichelo in the Guildhall (London).

3. Exterior from the South-East, *c.* 1819 –   – From an engraving by W. Pearson; from Clarke's *Architectura Ecclesiastica Londini.*

4. Exterior from the East, *c.* 1837 –   –   – From an engraving by Billings and Le Keux in Godwin's *Churches of London.*

5. Exterior from the East, *c.* 1837 –   –   – From the original pencil drawing for Plate 4 by R. W. Billings in the London County Council Collection.

6. Interior from the West, *c.* 1837 –   –   – From an engraving by Billings and Le Keux in Godwin's *Churches of London.*

7. Interior from the West, *c.* 1837 –   –   – From the original pencil drawing for Plate 6 by R. W. Billings in the London County Council Collection.

8. Exterior from the North-West, 1884 –   – From a water-colour drawing by J. P. Emslie in the London County Council Collection.

PHOTOGRAPHS AND DRAWINGS

9. The Ground Plan of the Church –   –   – From a measured drawing by the late J. L. Pearson, R.A., traced and re-arranged by P. K. Kipps.

10. Exterior, North Elevation –   –   –   – From a measured drawing by the late J. L. Pearson, R.A., traced by J. W. Bloe.

11. Exterior from the North-East, *c.* 1910 – – Photograph by Will F. Taylor.
12. Exterior from the North-West, 1928 – – Photograph by J. W. Bloe.
13. Tower from the North, *c.* 1910 –   – Photograph by Will F. Taylor.
14. Exterior, South Elevation –   –   –   – From a measured drawing by the late J. L. Pearson, R.A., traced by E. A. R. Rahbula.

PLATE

15. Exterior from the South-East, 1926   –   –   Photograph by Edward Yates.
16. South Porch and Turret Stair, c. 1863   –   –   Photograph lent by Dr. Philip Norman.

17. Exterior, East Elevation ⎫
18. Exterior, West Elevation ⎭   –   –   –   –   { From measured drawings by the late J. L. Pearson, R.A., traced by P. K. Kipps.

19. Old and New Ceilings, c. 1770   –   –   –   From an original pencil sketch by John Carter in the London County Council Collection.

20. Interior looking East, c. 1875   –   –   –   Photograph in the London Survey Committee Collection.

21. Interior Transverse Section looking East –   –   From a measured drawing by the late J. L. Pearson, R.A., traced by P. K. Kipps.

22. Interior looking East, c. 1910   –   –   –   Photograph by Will F. Taylor.
23. Interior looking East, 1926   –   –   –   –   Photograph by Edward Yates.
24. Interior Longitudinal Section looking North   –   From a measured drawing by the late J. L. Pearson, R.A., traced by P. K. Kipps.

25. Nave looking East, showing North Arcade, 1927   Photograph by J. W. Bloe.
26. North Aisle looking East, c. 1910   –   –   –   Photograph by Will F. Taylor.
27. North Chancel Aisle looking East, c. 1910   –   Photograph by Will F. Taylor.
28. South Aisle from the North Aisle, c. 1910   –   Photograph by Will F. Taylor.
29. East End of the Chancel Arcades, c. 1910   –   Photograph by Will F. Taylor.
30. Chancel and Nave Arcades from the North-East, c. 1910   –   –   –   –   –   –   –   Photograph by Will F. Taylor.
31. South Arcade, showing junction of styles –   –   Photograph by J. J. Edmunds.
32. (a) Bases to pier at junction of styles   –   –   Photograph by Francis R. Taylor.
    (b) Bases to piers, South Chancel Arcade   –   Photograph by J. J. Edmunds.
33. South Aisle looking East, c. 1910   –   –   –   Photograph by Will F. Taylor.
34. South Aisle looking West, c. 1910   –   –   Photograph by Will F. Taylor.
35. South Chancel Aisle, c. 1910 –   –   –   Photograph by Will F. Taylor.
36. Organ and Churchwardens' Pews, 1927 –   –   Photograph by J. W. Bloe.
37. Crypt looking West, 1927   –   –   –   –   Photograph by J. W. Bloe.
38. Crypt looking East, 1928   –   –   –   –   Photograph by J. W. Bloe.

FITTINGS

39. (a) Alms Box from Christ's Hospital   –   –   Photograph by J. J. Edmunds.
    (b) Post-Restoration Chair   –   –   –   Photograph by J. J. Edmunds.
40. Details of Benches   –   –   –   –   Measured drawing by E. F. Hervey.
41. Cistern in Tower   –   –   –   –   Photograph by Francis R. Taylor.
42. Communion Plate   –   –   –   –   Photograph by J. W. Bloe.
43. Communion Rail   –   –   –   –   Measured drawing by A. B. Waters.
44. Communion Rails   –   –   –   –   Photograph by J. J. Edmunds.
45. Communion Table   –   –   –   –   Photograph by Francis R. Taylor.

PLATE

46. Doorcase, North Entrance — — — — Measured drawing by J. F. Learner.

47. Details of Plate 46 — — - — — Measured drawing by J. F. Learner.

48. Doorway to North Porch — — — — Photograph by Edward Yates.

49. Doorway to Turret Stairs — — — — Photograph by Edward Yates.

50. Altar Tomb in South Aisle — — — — Photograph by Edward Pady.

51. Font and Enclosure — — — — — Measured drawing by G. Gordon Godfrey and Percy W. Lovell.

52. Font and Enclosure — — — — — Photograph by Francis R. Taylor.

53. Font and Cover — — — — — — Photograph by J. J. Edmunds.

54. Font-cover, looking to face of Dove — — Photograph by *Country Life*.

55. Font-cover, looking to back of Dove — — Photograph by Will F. Taylor.

56. 17th-Century Glass Panel — — — — From a drawing by F. S. Eden.

57. Iron Frame and Pegs — — — — — Measured drawing by Percy W. Lovell.

58. Iron Frame and Pegs — — — — — Photograph by Edward Yates.

59. The Organ Case — — — — — — Measured drawing by G. Gordon Godfrey and Percy W. Lovell.

60. General view of Organ and Gallery — — — Photograph by Francis R. Taylor.

61. Detail view of Organ Case — — — — Photograph by Francis R. Taylor.

62. Stuart Coat on Organ Gallery — — — Photograph by Francis R. Taylor.

63. Staircase to Organ Gallery — — — — Measured drawing by Francis R. Taylor.

64. Detail of Stairs under Organ Gallery — — Photograph by Francis R. Taylor.

65. Piscina in East Wall — — — — — Photograph by J. J. Edmunds.

66. Pulpit — — — — — — — — From a measured drawing by the late E. A. Rickards.

67. Detail of Handrail to Pulpit — — — — From a measured drawing by the late Bailey Scott Murphy.

68. Pulpit from the South-West — — — — Photograph by *Country Life*.

69. Pulpit, showing handrail and reading desk, *c.* 1910 Photograph by Will F. Taylor.

70. Carved Panel and Console to Pulpit Stairs, 1928 Photograph by Francis R. Taylor.

71. Reredos — — — — — — — Measured drawing by A. B. Waters.

72. Details of Reredos — — — — — Drawn by G. Gordon Godfrey.

73. Reredos, North Side — — — — — Photograph by Francis R. Taylor.

74. Reredos, South Side — — — — — Photograph by Francis R. Taylor.

75. Console Panels in Reredos — — — — Photographs by Francis R. Taylor.

76. Detail of Screens — — — — — — Photograph by *Country Life*.

77. Panelling enclosing Pews at West End of Nave Measured drawing by P. K. Kipps.

78. Carved Panels in Screen at West End of Nave — Measured drawing by P. K. Kipps.

79. The Sword-rests — — — — — — From a measured drawing by R. A. Rix and W. J. Bamber.

80. The Sword-rests, 1928 — — — — — Photograph by Edward Yates.

81. Sword-rest. Sir John Eyles — — — — Photograph by *Country Life*.

82. Sword-rest. Slingsby Bethell, Esq. — — Photograph by *Country Life*.

83. Sword-rest. Sir Thomas Chitty — — — Photograph by Francis R. Taylor.

84. West Window, North Aisle — — — — Photograph by J. J. Edmunds.

PLATE

85.   Panels in Churchwardens' Seats.   The Evangel-
       ists — — — — — — — — — — —   Photograph by George Trotman.

86.   Panels in Churchwardens' Seats.   The Evangel-
       ists — — — — — — — — —   Photograph by George Trotman.

87.
88.
89.   Panels in Churchwardens' Seats — — — Photographs by George Trotman.
90.

HERALDIC ILLUSTRATIONS

1.   DIOCESE OF ROCHESTER.   *Argent a saltire gules charged with a scallop or.*

2.   BARKING ABBEY.   *Azure in chief three lilies argent and in base three roses or all within a border gules charged with roundels argent.*

3.   DIOCESE OF CANTERBURY.   *Azure an archbishop's staff or with its cross argent surmounted by a pall argent edged and fringed with gold.*

4.   CHICHELE.   *Or a cheveron between three cinqfoils gules.*

5.   TIPTOFT, EARL OF WORCESTER.   *Argent a saltire engrailed gules.*

6.   TATE.   *Six pieces or and gules with three Cornish choughs.*

7.   EVYNGAR.   *His merchant's mark as shown on a shield upon his monument.*

8.   WYNTER.   *Checky or and sable a fesse argent.*

9.   KNOLLYS.   *Gules a cheveron argent with three roses gules thereon.*

10.   CROKE.   *Azure a fesse engrailed ermine between three eagles or.*

11.   TONGE.   *Party . . . and . . . a fleur de lis and a border engrailed, also parted and perhaps countercoloured.   The colours are not known.*

12.   MONMOUTH.   *Azure a cinqfoil between two demilions passant or all between two flaunches argent each charged with a griffon azure.*

13.   THYNNE.   *Barry of ten or and sable.*

On Sword-rests.

14.   SIR JOHN EYLES, Lord Mayor, 1727.   *Argent a fesse engrailed with three fleurs de lis in the chief all sable.*

15.   SLINGSBY BETHELL, Esqr., Lord Mayor, 1755.   *Argent a cheveron between three boars' heads sable with a star or upon the cheveron.*

16.   SIR THOMAS CHITTY, Lord Mayor, 1760.   *Gules a cheveron ermine with three talbots' heads razed or in the chief.*

xiv

PREFACE

THIS is the second volume of the Survey of London to deal with a City parish, and like the first (the Parish of St. Helen, Bishopsgate) it is concerned with the parish church. The subject of this work shared with the Church of St. Helen the fortune of having escaped the Great Fire, and architecturally as well as historically takes a high place amongst the ecclesiastical monuments of London within the wall. All Hallows, in addition to being the subject of several papers and innumerable references in the histories of London, was, in 1864, treated individually in a Monograph by the Rev. Joseph Maskell, then curate.

The historical portion of the present volume is entirely the work of Miss Lilian J. Redstone, and in acknowledging her scholarly and admirably compiled contribution the Committee also wishes to place on record its indebtedness to the enthusiasm and co-operation of the present Vicar of All Hallows, the Rev. P. B. Clayton, the well-known Padre of " Toc H." It is not too much to say that but for Mr. Clayton the present volume could scarcely have been attempted. The original research that its production entailed had been already undertaken at his own personal charge, and was intended to have been part of a book published by himself. When for various reasons this scheme could not be fulfilled, Mr. Clayton unreservedly and most generously placed the whole of his material at the disposal of the Committee, with the result that is now apparent in these pages.

The Committee is, moreover, under an obligation, not only to Mr. Clayton and Miss Redstone, but to others who had already given help to them, namely to Mr. Cyril E. Power, who gave much assistance in regard to the history of the building and especially to the localisation of the various Chapels, and to Mr. Francis C. Eeles for a very careful revision of the manuscript, the addition of the footnotes initialled " F.E." and the transcription of the Inventory of 1452. In addition, the Committee wishes to acknowledge the help of several who contributed after it had taken over the actual completion of the work. Mr. Frank L. Pearson has kindly lent the original drawings prepared by the late Mr. J. L. Pearson, R.A., with the help of which members of the Survey Committee have made the drawings of the church published here; Mr. Will F. Taylor has given the splendid series of photographs of the church taken about 1910, and Mr. E. Hudson has allowed the use from *Country Life* of the photographs of the pulpit, font-cover, and two of the sword-rests. Acknowledgment is also made to Mr. A. B. Waters and Mr. J. F. Learner for placing at the Committee's disposal measured drawings of the reredos and the north porch and doorway; to Mrs. Catherine Murphy for permission to reproduce the drawing of the pulpit handrail by her husband, the late Mr. Bailey Scott Murphy, in *English and Scottish Wrought Ironwork*; to Mr. Reginald A. Rix for permission to include the drawings of the sword-rests that appeared in the *Architectural Association Sketch Book*, and to Mr. H. V. Lanchester for those of the pulpit by his partner, the late Mr. E. A. Rickards, which also appeared in the same series, the proprietors and publishers of which have lent every assistance to the Committee. Mr. F. Sydney Eden has again assisted the Committee by contributing the notes on the ancient stained glass, while the Rev. E. E. Dorling has supervised the heraldic descriptions and also prepared the drawings for the marginal shields.

In compiling this first volume of the Parish of All Hallows Barking the Committee has included all the records which concern the church, its fabric and furniture, and has separated them from the personal monuments and other memorials within its walls. A full record and description of these latter has been prepared and will be given in the second volume, which will deal with the area of the parish and its inhabitants in so far as they are connected with the architectural vestiges to be described.

THE PARISH OF ALL HALLOWS BARKING.—PART I

ALL HALLOWS CHURCH
IN 1597

THE PARISH OF ALL HALLOWS BARKING

I.—HISTORY OF THE CHURCH

1.—*Foundations*

The origin of All Hallows Barking by the Tower is enshrouded in the mists of the Saxon past.* No records exist to indicate when or by whom the church was founded, and the only clue to its origin which we possess consists in its title of " Barking." This it had at least as early as the 12th century, for it is referred to by Walter, Bishop of Rochester from 1147 to 1182, as " Berkyncherche."†

The title more than suggests an original connection with the Abbey of Barking, which later owned it intermittently for two and a half centuries ; and though proof unfortunately is wanting, we are probably justified in assuming that in its origin the church was an appanage of the Abbey.‡ If so, it had passed out of the hands of the nuns by the reign of Stephen, for the *Registrum Roffense*§ records the gift of it (" Berchinchechirche *in Londoniis* ") at some date after the Norman Conquest to the Cathedral Church of Rochester by a " worthy man " (*probus homo*) named Riculf and his wife Brichtwen. How they had acquired it, and in whose hands it had been before it came to theirs, history does not record.‖

The possession of the church " called Berchingchireche, with all its appurtenances " was confirmed to Rochester by Henry II, probably in 1181.¶ It was assigned to the sacrist of Rochester, and thus the 40d. which it paid at Michaelmas, Christmas, Easter and Midsummer, went for some generations towards the upkeep of vestments, relics and holy vessels at Rochester.**

Diocese of Rochester

* The Roman pavement discovered under the tower (see p. 60) indicates that a part of the site, at any rate, was occupied by some kind of Roman building.
† *Registrum Roffense* (ed. Thorpe), p. 10.
‡ The suggestion that the site of the church was one of the two holdings in the neighbourhood of London with which Bishop Erkenwald (the " Light of London ") endowed the Abbey upon its foundation is a tempting one; but it is very doubtful whether it can be sustained. One of these holdings is said to lie upon the London way (" supra vicum Lundoniae ") and possibly formed the Abbey's manor of Tyburn ; the other, which Erkenwald had received from King Wulfghar, is described as " by London " (" juxta Lundoniam "), *see* Dugdale, *Mon.* i, 439. To identify the latter with the site of All Hallows is a bold expedient in face of the fact that the latter could never at any time have been outside the City wall. Canon Benham's statement (*Old London Churches*, p. 35) that " he [Erkenwald] endowed it [the Abbey of Barking] with fifteen acres of land to the west of the Tower of London ; a church was built here, and the original cluster of cottages grew into an important place " goes far beyond the evidence.
§ Thorpe's edition, p. 117.
‖ It may be conjectured that it had been lost to the Abbey in those troublous times when the Danes burned the monastery, nuns and all, in A.D. 870 or in a later invasion, when the Abbess and her flock took refuge in London (*Victoria County Hist. Essex*, ii, 116). It seems just possible that the Abbess then pledged, or otherwise alienated, this property, in order to obtain ready money when her House was in need.
¶ Dugdale, *Mon.* i, 177.
** *Custumale Roff.* (ed. Thorpe), 13, 14.

2.—*Barking Abbey and the Church*

The nuns of Barking eventually recovered the church; how or when is not known. Possibly they had regained it before 1285, for in that year and the year following socage, or quitrent, was being paid to the Abbey from certain houses in the parish,* including "Stapledehall." Indeed, early in 1321, the Abbess tried to get still more rent, and sent her collector into the very refectory of the Crutched Friars, outside the northern limits of the parish, to distrain for rent. The friars took back by force the small bell which the collector seized, and brought an action against the Abbess, who lost the day, for the jurors swore that no rent was due to her from the site of that House.† In 1291 the Abbess was receiving a pension of 6s. 8d. out of the church,‡ and her right of presentation was certainly established by 1303, when the advowsons belonging to Barking Abbey in the city were returned as those of St. Margaret Lothbury and All Saints of Berkyngechirche.§

Barking Abbey

The profits of the church were allocated to the chambress of the Abbey. For many years she can scarcely have relied with any sense of security upon the moneys from All Hallows. The near neighbourhood of the royal residence in the Tower and the popularity of the free chapel of St. Mary annexed to the church, made successive kings of England cast an envious eye upon it. Edward III got from the Abbey a grant of the advowson of All Hallows with a view to appropriating the church to a college of chaplains which he was projecting in the chapel of St. Peter ad Vincula within the Tower. He obtained from Pope Innocent VI a licence to this effect in 1355,‖ and compensated the Abbess by arranging for her a similar licence to appropriate the church of Tollesbury.¶ Edward III appointed Thomas de Broke as chaplain of St. Peter's and rector of All Hallows,** but the college of St. Peter's was never founded, and some thirty years later (1385) Richard II restored All Hallows church to Barking Abbey. At the same time, he gave the Abbess licence to appropriate the issues of the living††; accordingly succeeding incumbents were styled vicars, and the Abbey thenceforward took a larger proportion of the church profits. This recovery of the church cost the Abbey 20 marks (£13.6.8.), and was almost overthrown by Henry IV in 1402. He then appointed a warden to the chapel of St. Peter in the Tower, and granted him the parish church and chapel of Berkyng by the Tower. Whereupon the Abbess appeared in Chancery and, after long discussion, proved her contention that the church with its chapel was hers

---

* *Husting R. D. Enr.*, 16 (56), 24 (38).
† *Assize R.*, 546 m. 50 *d.*
‡ *Tax. Eccles. P. Nich.* (Rec. Com.), 19.
§ *Liber Custumarum* (Rolls Ser.), ii, 235.
‖ *Cal. Papal Letters*, iii, 562.
¶ *Cal. Pat.*, 1351–58, p. 155.
** *Ibid.*, 1361–64, p. 383; Newcourt, *Repertorium Ecclesiasticum* (ed. Hennessy), liv *n.*, f. 32.
†† *Cal. Pat.*, 1385–89, p. 43.

THE PARISH OF ALL HALLOWS BARKING

by Richard II's grant.* Once more, in 1485, the King compelled the Abbey to give up the church. The free chapel of St. Mary had by that date become the royal chantry of Edward IV, and Richard III set about erecting it into a deanery, to which the advowson of All Hallows should be appropriated. Richard's death put an end to this scheme for handing over the mother church to her daughter chapel shortly after the Abbess had made an (incomplete) surrender of the church, and Richard's nominee, Dr. William Talbot, had obtained a licence as " rector " to settle an annuity of £15 out of the church upon the Abbess and her successors.† Richard being dead, and Henry VII safely seated on the throne, the Abbey petitioned for the restoration of the church, and regained it,‡ holding it undisturbed until the Reformation. Then, in 1539, the Abbey of Barking with all its property was surrendered to the commissioners of Henry VIII.§ In 1542 Hugh Fuller, an auditor of the Court of Augmentations, and William Pownsett presented a vicar,‖ possibly on behalf of the Crown. The next presentation was made by the Archbishop of Canterbury in 1565.¶ He had evidently acquired the advowson by exchange with the Crown,** and the Archbishop again presented in 1585. Since then the patronage has remained with the Archbishops of Canterbury.

Diocese of Canterbury

3.—*The Dedication of the Church*

The old name of " Berkingchurch " clung to the building down to the beginning of the 16th century, when the present style of " All Hallows Barking " began to come into more general use. The church had a double dedication, to the Virgin Mary and to All Saints. Husband and wife would call their parish church by either name, indiscriminately. Thus Aleyn Johnson (a citizen and grocer, who for his soul's sake bequeathed all his wearing apparel to be sold, for the needy poor) desired to be buried in the " church of Alhalowen of Berkyngcherch " (1456),†† while his widow Elizabeth was buried in the same grave in the " parish church of Our Lady of Berkyng."‡‡ There is record of the dedication to Our Lady in 1281§§; and this was possibly the older invocation of the two and may have fallen into disuse later, to avoid confusion with the chapel of Our Lady in the church-

---

* *Ibid.*, 1401–5, p. 490.
† *Ibid.*, 1476–85, p. 470.
‡ *Ibid.*, 1485–94, pp. 326–27.
§ *L. & P. Hen. VIII*, xiv (ii), 519.
‖ Bonner 142.
¶ Grindall 137. Hennessy (*Nov. Rep.*, 74) gives Fuller and Pownsett as patrons in 1565 also ; but this disagrees with the Archbishop's Register.
** Hennessy gives the grant to the Archbishop as occurring in 1546 ; but this seems to arise from confusion with All Hallows the Great (*ad fenum*) which he acquired by exchange in that year. (P.R.O., *Partrs. for Grants*, 235.)
†† *Comm. Lond.*, 222 Sharp.
‡‡ *Ibid.*, 369 Wilde.
§§ *Hust. R.*, 12 No. 89.

3

yard, or " Berkingshaa." Reference has been found in one instance to " the parish of St. Mary le Chapel in All Hallows Barking."*

All Hallows was a favourite dedication with Londoners, who had ten or a dozen churches of this dedication. The parishioners of All Hallows Barking kept up the customs of their patronal feast even after the Reformation. Among the letters in the church chest is one written by John Godfrey of Crawley in Witney, co. Oxon., on 29th October, 1615, to his very loving sister Elizabeth Goddard at the lower end of Tower Street against Barking church, accompanying a cake for her and her friend " to tast of this Alhollen Day." This was probably one of the triangular " soul cakes," made either of aniseed or oats, which were generally given by the rich to the poor on the eve of All Souls' Day to encourage prayers for the departed.

Before the Reformation there were in the church various symbols of its dedication. In 1506 the church goods included " j awtyr cloythe for abovfe and beneythe of gren bavdkyne w^t Allhallowe there on." Moreover, the accounts for pulling down the rood in 1559–60 include 2od. " to a Carpenter for takinge downe of the Crucyfix, the Marye and John and alhallowes the patrone."† This was doubtless some symbolical figure resembling one still in existence in Westminster Abbey, which shows a bearded man in armour, wearing over it mass vestments representing all orders of clergy, and over them again the monastic hood and scapular. This figure with its beard symbolising the agricultural class, its armour the knight, and its garments the clergy, denotes that saintliness is found in every walk of life. At its feet is a dragon tied round the neck with a stole, a symbol of spiritual life overcoming sin.‡

4.—*The Church and the City*

All Hallows played an important part in the medieval life of the city. At nightfall common citizens, below the rank of the great lord or " substantial person of good reputation," hastened home to lay down their arms, when curfew rang out from St. Martin's le Grand, St. Lawrence Jewry or All Hallows " of Berkyngchirche." If they were found armed in the streets after the bell had rung, they were seized and thrown into the " Tun " in Cornhill, there to await with other " night-walkers " the Mayor's judgment on the following day.§

The position of the church close to the city boundary next the Tower gave it especial prominence, particularly when the King's justices visited the Tower to hold pleas of the crown for the city. Then, in the morning, upon warning given, all the citizens were bound to gather at

* *Pleas of Nuisance* (Guildhall Records Office), Roll DD.
† See below, p. 38.
‡ The suggestion that this figure represented All Saints was made by the late Mr. J. T. Micklethwaite in *Archæologia*, XLVII, 483–85 ; but a more recent authority [*R. Comm. on Hist. Monuments (England)*: *London*, i, Plate 211] describes it as St. Armagilus.
§ *Liber Albus* (Rolls Ser.), 275.

THE PARISH OF ALL HALLOWS BARKING

" Berkingecherche," clad well and respectably, fresh from the barber's hands, and with their hair newly trimmed. Whilst they waited at the church, a deputation of about half a dozen of the most respected citizens bearing gifts in their hands went forward to the Tower to welcome the King, his Council and the Justices, and to make it clear that in appearing before the royal justices they were not prejudicing their ancient liberties. This being allowed, and the judges' commission read, proclamation was made for the sheriffs of London. Whereupon, the Mayor, Aldermen and Sheriffs with a great crowd of citizens would enter the Tower from the church. On one occasion, probably in 1285, the Mayor, Gregory de Rokesley, took offence at some failure to give due respect to these ancient rights, and as a protest, he went to All Hallows church with all the city insignia, and there in the presence of between eighty and ninety citizens deposed himself, laying aside the symbols of his mayoralty and handing over the common seal to one of the aldermen, Stephen Aswey [Eswy]. Then with the rest he entered the Tower as a simple alderman. Edward I was quick to punish such disrespect. The citizens who were present at the Mayor's resignation in All Hallows were for a few days imprisoned in the Tower; Aswey was carried off to Windsor for a longer term; the King, finding London without a mayor, seized the city into his own hands* and kept it for thirteen years, until, faced by a combination of the barons and the Londoners, and gratified by the citizens' generous grant towards his Scottish wars, he restored the city's franchises in 1298. Upon another occasion in 1321, the judges at the Tower took umbrage at the delay in the arrival of the sheriffs, although it was in accordance with ancient custom that they had waited at the church to hear the answer to the first deputation of citizens. Again the King seized the city; but this time it was restored in a few months in view of an insurrection in Wales.†

5.—*Sanctuary* ‡

Knives were often out in the city during the Middle Ages, and on several occasions men flying from the hue and cry took refuge in All Hallows church. On Sunday, 7th September, 1325, two Flemings, Nicholas Crabbe and John Paling, started quarrelling on the Wool Wharf, within the parish. Nicholas first drew his knife, wounding John four times in the throat and forcing him towards the water's edge with intent to kill. At length, John got out his knife, called a " trenchour," and struck Nicholas to the heart so that he died. John the Waterbearer and John Whitehead standing by raised the alarm, and John Paling fled to the church for sanctuary. Next day the coroner and sheriffs came and parleyed with him in the church. He confessed that he had killed Nicholas, but refused to come out and take his trial. A fortnight later he died in the church of his wounds, whilst the sheriffs' officers watched the building to prevent his escape. Possibly his death was hastened

---

* *Annales Londonienses* (Rolls Ser.), 94 ; cf. *French Chron. of London* (Camden Soc.), 19.
† *Liber Custumarum* (Rolls Ser.), 289.
‡ Sharpe, *Cal. of City Coroners' Rolls, passim.*

by starvation, for the jurors returned that Nicholas had no goods at all, while John had only a surcoat and a shirt, which they valued at 6d.

Nicholas Motoun of Bristol, a porter, who killed John Croucheman, another porter, in Chickenlane just after curfew on Friday, 16th June, 1338, was more fortunate. He took refuge in the church close by, and there, about a week later, confessed the murder before the coroner and sheriffs; but they could not touch him while he remained in sanctuary, and afterwards he escaped by night.

Little more than a year later, Peter Tremenel, a servant of the household of Queen Philippa, took refuge in the church. On Friday, 23rd August, 1340, he had been quarrelling in the Tower with one of the Queen's grooms of the kitchen, John Gremet. At the hour of Vespers they were outside the Tower Postern on the river bank, when John drew a long knife and wounded Peter in three places. Thereupon Peter struck John in the throat with a short knife, so that he died that same day. Peter took sanctuary in All Hallows church, and next day confessed to the coroner and sheriffs what he had done, saying that he was so badly wounded that he could not leave the church except at risk of death, and that upon recovery he would submit and take his trial. His fate is unknown; but the jurors returned that he did appear to be very badly wounded. His adversary was buried in the church.

6.—*The Trial of the Templars*

Some of the most dramatic scenes in the suppression of the Order of the Knights' Templars took place within All Hallows church. The fall of Acre had set an end to the hopes of recovering the Holy Land, and therefore to the prime reason for the existence of a body of knights pledged to fight for the Holy Sepulchre. Their pride, the wealth of their Order and their growing intervention in the politics of their own countries brought upon them general jealousy and hatred. Urged by the Pope, and following the example of Philip of France, Edward II first arrested the Templars all over England (January, 1308) and seized their lands, and then tried to get evidence of the charges of blasphemy and heresy, which had been trumped up against them. Brother William de la More, Grand Preceptor of England, and many others were imprisoned in the Tower. The first connection of All Hallows parish with the proceedings against them occurred when all the English brethren were still maintaining their innocence after nearly two years' imprisonment. From October, 1309, onwards they were closely examined, generally in Holy Trinity Priory, but on one day in November four brethren, Robert de la Wolde, William de Cestreton, Alexander de Bulbecke and William de Welles, made their depositions in the chapel of the Blessed Mary of Berkyngecherche, before a number of friars.* They admitted none of the charges against the Order, to which they had belonged for periods ranging from 18 to 32 years. Again on 27th January, 1310, three others

* Wilkins, *Concilia*, ii, 345.

were examined in the same chapel, including a chaplain of the Order, John de Stoke, who was particularly examined as to a charge that Walter le Bacheler, Grand Preceptor of Ireland, had been starved to death.* John de Stoke described how he had helped to bury the Preceptor at dawn in a grave outside the graveyard of the Temple, since he was considered excommunicate for taking the goods of his house without acknowledging his fault. Many such examinations produced no English evidence against the Templars until Edward II gave way to papal admonitions, and in 1310 sent orders to the Tower to allow a restricted use of torture in order to extort confession from the Templars imprisoned there. Meantime, much hearsay evidence was gathered from the knights' enemies and read before them (22nd April, 1311). A week later the Grand Master, with two other prisoners in the Tower, was brought before the papal inquisitors and the bishops of London and Chichester in All Hallows church. There they formally presented their written answer to these allegations, ratifying what they had already declared to the officers of the Tower. They pleaded that they were all Christians, believing as Holy Church taught; that their religion was founded on vows of obedience, chastity and poverty, and of aiding in the conquest of the Holy Land; and that they were innocent of heresy and evil doing. For the love of God, and for charity, they besought their judges for trial as true children of the Church, and in accordance with the privileges granted by the court of Rome to their Order, so that they might bring forward Christian witnesses to speak to the manner of their lives. They ended by declaring their belief in the sacraments, and praying their judges to judge them as they themselves would answer before God; desiring that their examinations should be held in public and recorded in the very language and words in which they were given.†

The only answer to this dignified petition was a fresh order for the separate confinement of the prisoners and the application of unrestricted torture. At length, in July 1311, three of their number admitted the charges against them, and many others (with the notable exception of the Grand Preceptor) made public confession and were reconciled to the Church at high mass in St. Paul's. But five were too aged and impotent to make the journey, and these were reconciled to the Church in the chapel of St. Mary in All Hallows churchyard. Soon after sunrise on Tuesday, 5th July, 1311, the bishops of London, Chichester and Winchester came to the chapel, accompanied by a great crowd of citizens. The five old men were brought before them by officers of the Tower, abjured the heresies laid to their charge, and begged with tears to be admitted to Holy Church. Some spoke in French, others in English, the only tongue they knew. Then they made private confession to two masters of theology, and were absolved outside the west door of the chapel by the bishop of Chichester. Whereupon, the bishop led them into the chapel and up to the altar, where they knelt and prayed, devoutly kissing

---

* *Ibid.*, 346; Stoke was among those who in the end confessed (under torture) that they had denied Christ (*ibid.* 383 *et seq.*).

† *Ibid.*, 364.

the altar, and weeping the while. Afterwards they were sent to do penance among their enemies in various monasteries throughout the kingdom.*

7.—*The Church and Chancery*

In December 1323, another inquisition was held in the church of " All Hallows in Berkyngecherche." The city had wavered between Edward II and the Earl of Lancaster, until, deciding for the King, they sent an armed force which helped to decide the Earl's defeat at Boroughbridge. Nevertheless they were suspected of aiding Jacominus Darynoun and other adherents of the rebels. A commission out of Chancery was issued to the Mayor, Hamon de Chigwell, and another. They inquired into the matter by a London jury on Friday before the Circumcision, 1323, in All Hallows church. The jurors declared that no help had been given by the city for Jacominus and the rest, but that they had been received south of the river by the alien Prior of Bermondsey, who was accordingly committed to the Tower.†

At this period, the court of Chancery was held in no fixed place, and upon more than one occasion its routine business was conducted at the chapel in All Hallows churchyard. For instance, on 15th April, 1337, Margaret de Bacheworth came into Chancery at " Berkyng chapel " and acknowledged a deed which she had made touching a certain manor near St. Albans.‡ The church and chapel seem to have been used indiscriminately for such purposes. At midnight 30th November, 1340, Edward III returned unexpectedly to the Tower, angry with the Lord Chancellor for failing to send him those supplies which should have enabled him to follow up his victory at Sluys in the previous summer. Arriving in no good humour after a stormy three days' passage, the King received the chancellor, Robert bishop of Chichester, in his chamber at the Tower and took from him the great seal which had been in use in England, handing it to William de Kildesby. Much business was left to be transacted both with this seal, and with another which the King had had with him in France and had placed in a bag sealed with his own (privy) seal. Accordingly, on the following Saturday, at the hour of evensong, Kildesby took both of the great seals to the " church of Berkyng near the Tower " and caused the bags containing them to be opened there before the chief barons of the Exchequer and certain clerks in Chancery. The writs already dated in England were sealed with the one seal; charters made by the King beyond the sea were sealed with the other. Then the seals were replaced in their bags and taken back to the King at the Tower. On Thursday, 14th December, Edward gave the seal to Sir Robert Bourchier, the first layman to hold office as chancellor. On the Friday the new chancellor took the seal to " Berkyngchapel next the Tower," opened the bag in which it was and sealed writs there, receiving also the acknowledgment of the Prior of St. John of Jerusalem who came in person to make recognisance of a deed

---

* Wilkins, *Concilia*, ii, 391.
† *Chancery Inq., Misc.*, File 93 (31); *Cal. Pat.*, 1321–24, p. 358.
‡ *Cal. Close Rolls*, 1333–37, p. 660.

8

granting certain yearly pensions. Next day (Saturday, 16th December) Bourchier was setting out on a journey on his own affairs, and accordingly sent the great seal to the King, who was sitting at dinner in his chamber at the Tower, when a clerk of chancery brought it to him. This clerk, Sir Edmund de Grymesby, and another, Thomas de Brayton, were ordered to deliver it to Thomas de Evesham. Again they did so at " Berkyngchapel," delivering it to Evesham, who carried it thence to his house in Fetter Lane.*

8.—*The Royal Lady Chapel*

There stood within the churchyard of All Hallows the chapel of Our Lady (*see* p. 2), which is said to have been founded by Richard Cœur de Lion, and was certainly erected into a royal chantry-chapel by Edward IV.

The earliest known record of such a chapel is the will[†] of Edward Grobbe who, about 1278, left his ship, the *Blewebolle*, to be sold for the maintenance of a chantry in the chapel of St. Mary de Berkinggechirch; but it is just possible that he intended the Lady Chapel, which is known to have existed in the south aisle of the church and was quite distinct from the Lady Chapel in the churchyard. In 1297 Richard de Glamuile broke into the chapel of " Berkyngchirch " and stole a " coronele " of pearls, three gold rings, a linen cloth, an embroidered frontal and certain ornaments of the church; for which deed he was hanged, while one of the parishioners, Geoffrey le Hurer, who had prosecuted, recovered the goods for the use of the church.[‡] Peter Blakeney of Mark Lane, who in 1310 desired to be buried in All Hallows church, left money to the chapel of St. Mary *by* that church.[§] The trial and submission of the Templars in the chapel in 1309 and 1311 has been noted. The rector of All Hallows, Walter Grapenel, who had been presented to the living by Edward II during a voidance of Barking Abbey, was styled " warden of Berkyngchapel, London " when in 1328 he was charged with aiding in the breaking of a close at Wratting, co. Suffolk, and in assaulting servants and carrying away goods.[||] The use of this chapel for purposes of state is recorded in 1336 and again in 1337, when deeds were acknowledged in Chancery " at Berkyngchapel, London," and it has already been related how Sir Robert Bourchier sealed certain writs with the great seal there upon his appointment as Chancellor in 1340. The style used in naming the church shows how highly the chapel stood in men's minds. Thus, the Controller of the Household of Edward III's children, in paying for the funeral of John Gremet, groom of the kitchen, who had been slain in 1340 by Peter Tremenel, speaks of him as buried *in ecclesia de Berkyng Chapelle*.[¶] Thomas Pilkes, founder of a chantry in the church of All Hallows,

---

* *Ibid.*, 1339–41, pp. 649, 653, 656.
† *Husting R.*, 9, No. 20.
‡ *Goal Delivery R.*, 37.
§ *Husting R.*, 40, No. 26.
|| *Cal. Pat.*, 1327–30, p. 282.
¶ *Excheq. K. R.*, Accts. Var. 389, No. 11.

c

desired in 1348 to be buried within the churchyard *near* the chapel of St. Mary de Berkinge near the Tower.* In 1359, Denys de Morbek, a knight who had been concerned in the capture of the French king at Poitiers, was lying like to die at his lodging in a street by the church called Berkyng Chapelle.† Richard Amuresden, a chaplain, on his death-bed in May 1385 desired to be buried in the chapel of the Blessed Mary of Berkyng, London;‡ and in the same year certain houses in Chickenlane were said to abut upon the chapel called Berkyngchapel on the west.§ It has already been seen how Henry IV tried to annex the chapel, as well as the church, to S. Peter's in the Tower.

Chichele

Attached to the chapel was a gild or brotherhood " in worship of the Blessed Virgin Mary," which is said to have been founded by Thomas Chichele, probably the father of Henry Chichele, Archbishop of Canterbury, who founded All Souls' College, Oxford, and of Sir Robert Chichele, friend of Richard Whittington and twice Mayor of London. Thomas Chichele was buried at Higham Ferrers, co. Northants, in 1400; and the Chichele rents with which he apparently endowed the fraternity were with other properties subject to a yearly payment to All Souls' College towards an obit for Sir Robert Chichele.‖ The earliest record found of this brotherhood is the will of one of the shipwrights of Pety Wales, John Rolff, a citizen of London. In May 1432 he desired that his lighter *le John* should be sold to perform his will, which included a bequest of 6s. 8d. to the brotherhood of the Blessed Mary in the chapel of the Blessed Mary by (*iuxta*) the church of All Hallows.¶ About this time, the chapel, like the church itself, seems to have been undergoing considerable repair, for in 1410, Simon Hugh, citizen and woolman, bequeathed 40s. to the fabric of the chapel, where it was most needed. This was one of numerous bequests for the good of his soul, for which his executors were to hasten to have 3000 masses celebrated immediately after his death. He also endowed a chaplain to celebrate for seven years both in the church and the chapel, and to be in the church at all canonical hours, also celebrating a trental (thirty masses) of St. Gregory during the first year after Hugh's death.** John Cok, a citizen and clothier, who was buried in the churchyard at the east end of the church in 1440, also gave 40s. to the fraternity of the Blessed Virgin Mary in the chapel of the Blessed Virgin in the churchyard to pray for his soul.†† Another chaplain, William Heth, was buried in the chapel of the Blessed Virgin Mary near the church in 1452, and gave 6s. 8d. to the works of the chapel.‡‡ Sibyl Salueyn, who was buried there in 1453, provided for a chaplain to celebrate there, and for the good

---

* *Husting R.*, 78, No. 251.
† *Cal. Pat.*, 1358–61, p. 320.
‡ *Comm. Lond.*, 129 Courtney.
§ *Anct. Deed* (P.R.O.), A. 1650.
‖ *Augm. Off., Partrs. for Grants*, 2114.
¶ *Husting R.*, 162, No. 16.
** *Comm. Lond.*, 174 Broun.
†† *Ibid.*, 44 Prowet.
‡‡ *Ibid.*, 25 Sharp.

friendship shown her by the vicar bequeathed him a silver cup with a cover.*
Sir John Vale, one of the chaplains of Pilkes' chantry in All Hallows church,
desired in 1458 that two of the great waxlights of 4 lbs. each, which stood
about his body during his exequies, should afterwards remain in the chapel
of the Blessed Virgin Mary in the churchyard of the said church.†

By the middle of the 15th century, many generations of parishioners had thus contributed to the beautifying of the chapel, and there can be
no doubt that there was already set up in it a somewhat extraordinary image of
Our Lady. It may have been identical with " our lady Image of Barkyng,"
which in 1506 showed " a gracious miracle . . . by a mayeden child that
a cart Ladyn w^t stone yood over."‡ It was probably this same image which
stood on the north side of the chapel some fifty years later, when Robert Tate
founded his chantry there. The chapel was evidently gaining in popularity
when there were enrolled in the register of bishop Gilbert of London (1436–48)
certain letters§ which purported to be an indulgence of forty days granted on
20th May, 1291, by three papal legates to all who should visit the chapel in
the churchyard of Berking-Church, London, contribute to its lights, repairs or
ornaments, and pray for the soul of Richard, king of England, whose heart
this supposed indulgence stated to have been buried in the chapel beneath
the high altar. These letters bear many signs of such forgery as even the
highest ecclesiastics of the Middle Ages were wont to perpetrate. They may,
however, contain a grain of truth, for it is possible that (as the letters assert)
the chapel had been founded by Richard Cœur de Lion,‖ although his
heart was not buried there, and that the image was the gift of Edward I,
who was as greatly devoted to works of piety as he was to just administration
and statesmanship. No contemporary record of the connexion of either
king with the chapel has, however, yet been found.

The story of the image of St. Mary, *as it was accepted in the 15th
century,* ran as follows: In the time of Henry III the hostile Welsh over-
ran England, slaughtering men, women and even babes in the cradle.
At length they took the Isle of Ely and held it for a year, withdrawing to
Wales when it pleased them so to do. The young prince Edward was so
grieved at the disinheritance of his father and the ruin of his country, that he
took to his bed and thought never to recover. One night he prayed earnestly
to the Virgin Mary to show him how England could be speedily delivered
from the Welsh, whereupon as he slept the Virgin appeared to him in a vision,
saying, " O Edward, the friend of God, behold I am here. Know that during
thy father's life, the Welsh cannot be altogether overcome by the English,
because of thy father's great sin, and excessive extortions ; but go to-morrow

---

* *Ibid.,* 111 Sharp.

† *Ibid.,* 262 Sharp. It will be gathered from this and like evidence that the practice
of using dark-coloured or unbleached wax candles at requiem services was not followed in medieval
times, but that the same kind of wax was used for all purposes. (F. E.)

‡ Robert Fabyan, *Chronicles* (1811), p. 689.

§ See App. I below.

‖ No record of payments for the purpose has, however, been found upon the Pipe Rolls of
his reign.

morn to a certain Jew, Marlibrun by name, who is more skilled in the making of pictures than anyone in the whole world, and lives at Billinsgate in London. Cause him to make for thee an image in such shape as thou now seest me, and he by divine inspiration shall make two aspects in the one image, (*duas facies in una imagine*), one like unto my Son Jesus, the other he shall make beautiful like unto myself in all things, so that none can truthfully point out any defect. This image thou shalt have set up in the chapel in the churchyard of Berkyng-chirche by the Tower of London and shalt cause to be beautified there on the north side." She went on to tell the prince that Marlibrun himself and his wife, upon seeing the double aspect of the image in the chapel, should be turned to the Catholic faith and should reveal many secrets for which the Jews ought to be punished; that Edward himself should take a vow when he was in England to visit the image five times each year; that when his father was dead and he had become king he should overcome the Welsh, and should subjugate Scotland; and that every good king of England who should make a like vow and keep it to the best of his ability should be victorious over the Welsh and Scots and should be invincible.

The letters then declare that Edward I had of his own accord taken his oath before the magnates of England and Scotland; that everything which had been thus revealed to him in his sleep, had come to pass; and that accordingly the legates, wishing that the chapel should be frequented and revered, remit forty days of purgatory to those penitents who should visit it and aid it as described above, subject to confirmation by the Diocesan.

The alleged burial of Richard Cœur de Lion's heart beneath the chapel altar has no historic truth. When Richard died at Chaluz, his heart was carried to Rouen for burial, and was found in an inscribed casket there as recently as 1838.*

The letters of indulgence purport to have been dated at Norham, at the conference of the English and Scottish magnates touching the Scottish succession, 20th May, 1291. The declaration which they ascribe to Edward would have been in keeping with the claims to the overlordship of Scotland, which he then put forward. The story of the vision applies to the years 1267–69, when, after aiding his father to put down the Welsh and to reduce the disinherited magnates in the Isle of Ely in July 1267, Edward took an active part in promoting the statute of 1269, forbidding Jews to acquire the lands of Christians by means of pledges. Between these two events, in the spring of 1268, he had been appointed warden of London and custodian of all English castles, including the Tower. There may have been some basis of truth, therefore, in this account of his setting up an image in the chapel near the Tower; but it is impossible not to connect this picturesque document with the ingenious vicar, Thomas Virby, who was presented to All Hallows Church in 1434, and whose brass is still in the church.

Virby encouraged the people who thronged Tower Hill in the summer of 1440 to do honour to Richard Wyche, a Lollard vicar of Deptford,

* *Archæologia*, xxix, 205; cf. *Richard Cœur de Lion and the church of All Hallows Barking* by P. Norman, Trans. Lond. and Middx. Arch. Soc., 1923.

who had been burned on Tower Hill. Many men and women went to the hill by night, and offered at the place where Wyche had been burned money and images of wax, kneeling and making their prayers " as they would have done to a saint." Virby, as the parish priest, received their offerings and afterwards confessed in prison that to increase the people's fervour he had strewn ashes mingled with spice on the place of execution, so that the simple people were deceived " wenyng that the swete flauour hadde comme of the asshis of the ded heretic;"* for it was widely held that a sweet smell was among the many properties connected with relics of saints that were evidence of sanctity.† His servant also drew up a list of imaginary miracles which had been performed at the place. It therefore seems quite possible that the same servant was responsible for the curiously-worded indulgence which recites the legend of Our Lady's chapel; and that the Bishop was ready to countenance a diversion of popularity from the site of a Lollard's martyrdom to the neighbouring chapel of St. Mary.

9.—*Royal Charters and Statutes of the Fraternity of the Chapel*

It was within two years of Wyche's death, viz. on 9th January, 1442, that the fraternity of the Blessed Virgin in the chapel of the Blessed Mary within the churchyard of Berkyngechirche received from Henry VI a charter of incorporation. The King gave licence to his beloved lieges, Master John Somerset, Chancellor of the Exchequer; Henry Frowik; John Olney, Alderman of the City of London; John Merston, Clerk of the King's Jewels; Master William Clif, clerk; Thomas Walsingham, one of the customers of the Port of London; and to three city merchants, viz., Richard Riche, Thomas Canynges‡ and Hugh Withe, to establish such a fraternity and to admit therein brothers and sisters and to receive goods for it. Each year the fraternity might choose a master and four wardens. It was to be one commonalty and body in thing and in name, and to have a common seal and power to plead and be impleaded.

We know that a fraternity had already existed in the chapel, and it is clear that this royal charter of incorporation is closely connected with Bishop Gilbert's enrolment in his register of the alleged letters of indulgence. The royal charter continues to summarise the contents of that document. The King recites that he has learned of late that the chapel was wonderfully founded, built and established by the zeal of King Richard the First, out of his pure devotion; and that a certain image *still existing* in the chapel was miraculously and honourably placed there by the illustrious King Edward,

---

* *City Records. Journ.* iii, ff. 46, 47; cf. V. C. H., *London*, i, 222 and the references there cited.

† Resistance to ordinary corruption was another such property, and healing powers were another. F. E.

‡ Presumably the Thomas Canynges who sprang from the great merchant family of that name in Bristol and became Mayor of London in 1456 (Geo. Pryce, *Memorials of the Canynges Family*, pp. 143–46).

son of Henry the First (*Primi*) [*sic*, an obvious error], by reason of a divine revelation shown to that King in his sleep. Therefore, to secure the continuance of his predecessors' intent, Henry VI gave to the Master and Wardens and brothers and sisters of the fraternity the custody of the chapel, and the goods given for its use and adornment, but they were to keep the building in repair, and the parish church was still to receive the oblations made in the chapel.*

Edward III and Henry IV had both attempted to join All Hallows church with its Lady Chapel to their chapel of St. Peter within the Tower. Henry VI by this charter gave the chapel to the fraternity which was governed by officers of his own Court, headed by John Somerset, the physician and mathematician, who served as Chancellor of the Exchequer from 1441 to 1446. Edward IV followed yet another course, and in 1465 raised the Lady Chapel into the status of a royal chantry. The master of the fraternity, which governed the chapel, was then the King's own kinsman, John Tiptoft, earl of Worcester, a notable soldier and scholar, who in his travels had imbibed much of the new Italian learning and was connected with the neighbourhood as Constable of the Tower. Edward IV granted to Tiptoft, as master of the fraternity, and to its wardens Sir John Scot, Knt., Thomas Colt, John Tate and John Croke, the manor of Tooting Bec in Surrey, which had been seized by the Crown as the property of an alien priory. The fraternity was to use the profits of this manor for maintaining two chaplains, who should celebrate perpetually in the chapel for the welfare of Edward IV and his Queen, his mother Cecily, duchess of York, his brothers the dukes of Clarence and Gloucester, then still living, and for their souls after death, and for the souls of the King's father (Richard, late duke of York) and his dead brother the late earl of Rutland and of all the faithful departed, especially those Yorkists who had shed their blood in bringing Edward to the throne. The Master and Wardens were also to keep the building itself in repair out of the profits of the manor, and they and the brothers and sisters of the fraternity were to have the custody of the chapel for ever.†

The Statutes for this chantry, which were drawn up by the Master and Wardens in accordance with the King's instructions, are still in existence.‡ The chantry was to be called " King Edward's Chauntry." It was to consist of two chaplains, secular (*i.e.* not monastic), well-read and of good life and conduct, and not beneficed elsewhere nor having more than £3. 6s. 8d. a year of their own patrimony. They should be replaced, upon resignation or deprivation, by the unanimous choice of the fraternity who (if possible) should appoint graduates in sacred theology. They were to be admitted by the bishop and inducted by the archdeacon, and if the fraternity could not come to a unanimous choice within two months, the Master and two of the Wardens should appoint.

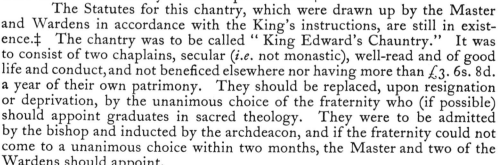

Tiptoft

* This charter has only been found recited in the confirmation by Henry VIII (*Pat. R.*, 6 Hen. VIII, pt. 1, m. 16).

† *Pat. R.*, 5 Edw. IV, pt. i, m. 19.

‡ *Excheq. T. R. Misc. Bk.*, 110.

THE PARISH OF ALL HALLOWS BARKING

The chaplains, if they were graduates and able to preach, should preach four times in the year on different days in the parish church. At these sermons, and at their masses and all other divine offices they were to remember in silence the founders who were still living, and after their death to make more particular, and public commendations for their souls. They were to say matins, evensong and the other canonical hours daily in the chapel, except upon Sundays and feast-days, when they were to take part in divine worship in the parish church, being present there in their surplices at the canonical hours, and at high mass to sing and take part in the celebration with the rest of the choir. On such days, they were to celebrate their own masses in the chapel one after the other at such convenient times as the vicar should choose; but he was not to prevent them from celebrating their masses directly after the singing of the gospel at high mass in the parish church.

On Sundays, Wednesdays and Fridays, they were to say "without note" the exequies (*exequias*) of the dead, lauds and commendations (*comendationes*) after the Sarum Use for the estate and souls of the founders. Clad in their surplices, they were to take part in every procession in the church or churchyard and in other general or solemn processions throughout the City, and in the singing of the anthem of Our Lady.

Every year the chaplains were to have a month's holiday, taken either continuously or piecemeal for their refreshment and to enable them to visit their friends or go on pilgrimage, but they were not to be away together, unless there were good reason, particularly at the great feasts, and the vicar was to arrange the date for their holiday. If one of them overstayed his leave by a fortnight, he had to show good reason for doing so before the bishop; if he overstayed it by two months, he was to lose his appointment. Otherwise his appointment was for life. If one of the chaplains became too aged or too sick to perform his office, he was to be removed, but was to enjoy his full salary in recompense for his prayers and other works of charity.

These statutes were drawn up by Tiptoft and the wardens, and two chaplains were appointed; but before the bishop had confirmed them (10 Dec., 1476) Tiptoft had himself lost his life in the Yorkist cause, being executed on Tower Hill during the short restoration of the Lancastrian King Henry VI in 1470. Edward IV after regaining his authority confirmed the fraternity in its possessions by specifically excepting Tooting Bec Manor from the Act of Resumption of Crown Lands in 1473.* Some difficulty afterwards arose from the stringent regulation in the statutes that each chaplain before his admission should hear them clearly and distinctly read, and should take an oath to keep them all. Accordingly, in 1485, the wardens of the fraternity, not wishing that the chaplains should incur the penalty of perjury for every slight deviation from the statutes, and possibly hoping thereby to augment the funds of the brotherhood, ordained a system of fines for absence, viz. 2d. for evensong, 3d. for matins, 1d. for procession,

* *R. of Parliament* (Rec. Com.), VI, 94.

4d. for high mass on Sundays and feast days in the church, 1d. for evensong, mass, matins, commemoration of the dead or the anthem of Our Lady in the chapel, and a fine for failure to preach, should the chaplain be a graduate in theology.*

Richard III's attempt to establish the chapel as a deanery with the Church of All Hallows attached came to nothing, but his successor (Henry VII) did not deprive the fraternity of its endowments. They were specifically excepted from the Act of 1485 whereby Henry resumed all lands alienated by Richard III,† and in 1490 the King confirmed the royal chantry as established by Edward IV. Shortly after the accession of Henry VIII, the fraternity once more sought the security of a royal charter, and in 1514 obtained from the new king a confirmation of Henry VI's charter of incorporation as well as of the later charter.‡ This royal protection, however, did not serve to exempt the chapel from the common fate which swept away all chantry chapels and colleges as superstitious uses in 1547.

We can get some idea of the chapel's appearance from contemporary record. The image of Our Lady stood to the north of the High Altar, the place usually occupied by the patron saint. John Barker, a merchant of Calais Staple, desired§ in 1500 to be buried " in the litle chapell where the ymage of our blissed lady of Barkyng in London stondeth." The description of the image as it was alleged to have been revealed to Edward I seems to apply to a statue of the Virgin carrying the Holy Child.|| There was in addition a " pictour of Jesus " before which John Kervyle, another merchant of Calais, desired to be buried in 1521.¶ He was to be " brought to earth " with sixteen wax torches and four wax tapers, borne about his hearse by twenty poor men of the parish. After his exequies, the torches were distributed to various churches, two going to All Hallows to burn " in honour of tholy sacrament at the tymes of Levacyon." For fifteen years after Kervyle's death, an " honest " priest sang for his soul at the altar of Our Lady, taking part also in all divine service in the parish church.

Tate

Most conspicuous in the chapel were two chantry tombs, the one of Sir Robert Tate, mercer and alderman of London, and Mayor in 1488, who lived in a " great messuage " in Tower Street,** the other of Sir John Rysley, Kt. The tomb of Sir Robert Tate lay " on the Northside of the same chapell before thymage of Oʳ Lady there and as nygh to the wall as convenyently may be." It may have stood within a small subsidiary chapel; for he left instructions†† that a " fayr and sufficient arche " should be cut in the North wall from East to West with a chapel, to be named St. Thomas'

* *Excheq. T. R. Misc. Bk.*, 110.
† *R. of Parliament* (Rec. Com.), VI, 343.
‡ *Pat. R.*, 6 Hen. VIII, pt. i., m. 16.
§ *P.C.C.*, 10 Moone.
|| *Duas facies in una imagine*, the one of the Virgin, the other of her Son Jesus.
¶ *P.C.C.*, 3 Ayloffe.
** *Ct. of Hustings, Deeds Enr.* R. 236, No. 23.
†† See App. II.

chapel, " convenient from the said arch toward the North as the ground there . . . reasonably may be sparyd." In the East end of this chapel of St. Thomas was an altar, where a priest sang for the souls of Sir Robert and his relatives and benefactors. In consideration of the making of this chapel of St. Thomas, the wealthy merchant gave £20 towards the repairs of the body of the Lady Chapel. He also made provision for " a table convenyent of seynt Thomas the martyr wᵗ his martyrdom therin conteyned to serve afore* the high awter " of the Lady Chapel. Apparently in addition to this altar-piece, his executors provided either over the altar of his chantry chapel of St. Thomas, or for the chantry which he established in St. Michael's, Coventry, his ancestral town, a finely-painted Flemish picture† of the Nativity in triptych form, the inner panels of the doors representing on the one side Sir Robert Tate kneeling,‡ on the other St. Joseph, or one of the shepherds, surmounted by the arms of Sir Robert, impaling those of his wife Margery (Wood). The outer panels of these doors represented St. Ambrose and St. Jerome.§

The Lady Chapel seems to have been in urgent need of repair when Tate's chantry was founded. One of the royal chaplains, Dennis Spicer, who in 1500 wished to be buried next Sir Thomas Salarse (probably a fellow-chaplain), before the entrance to the chapel choir, gave £5 to the chapel if the Fraternity took steps for its repair or rebuilding (*constructionem*) within three years. William Kirfote, a citizen and grocer who was to be buried on the north side of the Lady Chapel in 1514, gave 20s. for its repairs, and also left his tenements at Queenhithe to the vicar and churchwardens of All Hallows for a perpetual obit to be kept for him once a year within the chapel.‖ Sir Richard Cholmondeley, who also desired burial in the chapel, wished to lie " on thoder side agaynst where Sir John Rysley knt. lyeth buried," provided the Fraternity would agree.¶ Thus there was a knight's tomb on either side of the chapel.

---

* Usually the altar in England was a plain structure of stone covered with a textile frontal save in the last three days of Holy Week and at funerals. The word " afore " may indicate a reredos. But it may also mean a movable frontal of painted wood. The word, however, may be the error of a copyist in a somewhat carelessly registered will; in which case it probably stands for " above." F. E.

† Now in the possession of Millicent, Duchess of Sutherland.

‡ This is a suggestion only. Richard Corner (*Memorials of Persons interred in All Hallows, Barking;* Lond. and Middx. Arch. Soc., 11, 246) says that these are two of the Magi, the one holding a cap of maintenance.

§ Subsequent guesswork by Horace Walpole converted the two Fathers of the Church into portraits of Archbishop Kempe and Cardinal Beaufort, the latter " in the character he *ought to have* possessed, a pious contrite look." By a similar conjecture, the kneeling figure, more probably that of Sir Robert Tate, became Duke Humphrey of Gloucester, and all three figures were engraved as these characters for Harding's *Shakespeare* (1791–2).

‖ *P.C.C.,* 23 Holder.

¶ *Ibid.,* 22 Maynwaring.

10.—*Suppression of the Royal Chapel*

In 1547 " was Barkyng chappylle at the Towre hylle pullyd down,"* while the advanced party of the Reformation were suppressing all colleges and chantries, whether of royal foundation or no, and taking down all images, in their zeal for the prevention of " superstitious uses." The Master and Wardens of the Fraternity yielded up its goods reluctantly, and the royal commissioners were still without £29 in ready money, or the debenture for it, in November, 1557; but the suppression of the chapel was absolute. The royal chaplains, Sir John Aleyn, priest and Master of Arts, and John Wysdale, the chantry priest John Arley who sang for the soul of Sir John Rysley, and the chantry priest Richard Davyers who served in Sir Robert Tate's chapel of St. Thomas, went their ways. The royal commissioners took the three gilt chalices, which together weighed nearly 60 ounces, the parcel gilt pax, upon which the members of the Fraternity were wont to make their kiss of peace, the vestments of blue cloth of gold, red velvet, and white " satten of Bridges," the " paned " altar-cloths of red and blue and red and white, and the old altar-cloth of Baudkin. They took the chapel furniture down to the very least, the two pillows (or cushions for the books) one of red velvet the other of green damask, the pewter cruets and basons, the latten candle-sticks, the ten old candlestick bowls from the rood-loft, the four " old vestments very bad," the two old chests, and the little press " with a settell [of] pewes," the little table, and—what we should rejoice to see again—a great chest, bound with iron " wherein the evidence doe lye." They valued all this at £54 odd, over and above the money, plate and ornaments; the mass books were provided by the mother church.† Indeed the Fraternity had sometimes been put to it to find storage for their goods, and in 1500 had rented a house in Seething Lane " for laying of Our Lady Stuff."‡

The endowments of the chapel were also seized by the Crown. The manor of Tooting Bec with which Edward IV had endowed the Fraternity, was sold to John, earl of Warwick, for twenty-two years' purchase.§ Chichele's Rents in Tower Street, the original endowment of the Fraternity, producing £13 odd yearly, were first rated for a lease to Richard Drewe and Roger Wignall, watermen, and afterwards purchased by John Yelde, a woodmonger, and Nicholas Michell, a beerbrewer.‖ Tate's tenements were divided, and the one with shops, cellars and solars went to Henry Polsted of Chilworth and William More of Loseley Park in Surrey at eighteen years' purchase, subject to the tenancy of Ellen " Evinger,"¶ who must have been connected with John Evyngar, the brewer, who was buried

Evyngar

* *Chron. of the Grey Friars* (Camden Soc.), 55.
† Church Goods (Excheq. K. R.) 4, No. 1.
‡ *P.C.C.*, 15 Moone.
§ *V.C.H. Surr.*, IV, 95.
‖ *Augm. Off., Particulars for Grants*, 2114.
¶ *Ibid.*, 1887.

18

THE PARISH OF ALL HALLOWS BARKING

in All Hallows church. Bartholomew Compayne had a bargain, when he bought part of the endowment of Sir John Rysley's chantry, being a house in Broad Street in the parish of St. Christopher Stocks, which " by the King's pleasure " he was allowed to have at ten years' purchase.*

And what of the chapel itself? John Stow, writing at the end of the 16th century, says that it stood to the north of the church and " was pulled downe in the yeare 1548 . . . [and] the grounde was imployed as a Garden plot during the raigns of King Edward, Queene Mary, and parte of Queene Elizabeth till at length a large strong frame of Timber and bricke was set thereon, and imployed as a storehouse of Marchantes goodes brought from the sea by Sir William Winter."† William Wynter in 1562, before he was knighted, was rated in Seething Lane for 2s. 6d., next to his father George Wynter rated at 12d., these being the last two assessments in the lane. About 1576 Mr. George Wynter, who had come from Dyrham, co. Gloucestershire, was assessed in the lane for 2s. Perhaps (in view of the later history of the tenement) we may take it that the 12d. for which one Thomas " Bennye " (possibly for Beamontie) was rated represents his son's property; for while George Wynter himself occupied the one tenement, William let his part which was " one great warehouse " in Sethinge Lane to Hipolitan Beamontie, a merchant stranger. Subsequently Hipolitan rented George Wynter's tenement also, and in 1585, William Wynter sold to Richard Smythe, a citizen and fishmonger dwelling in Bow Lane, both the " messuage or tenement in Sethinge Lane in the parish of All Hallows Barking " and " the one great warehouse in the said lane and parish."‡

Wynter

From the deed of sale, we can reconstruct something of the story of the site between the demolition of the chapel and its acquisition by the Wynters, father and son. According to this deed, the messuage owned and occupied by George Wynter had previously been occupied by Robert Smythe. Now the tenement in Seething Lane which had been occupied by Robert Smythe had descended by May 1553 to Grace Smythe Widow, possibly his relict. She was then paying a yearly rent of 66s. 8d. for it, and this rent with the reversion on the termination of her lease had been acquired in the previous February by Thomas Vicarie, Edward VI's surgeon. Vicarie was to pay a yearly rent or farm to the Crown and in May 1553 Thomas Reve and George Cotton applied for permission to purchase this farm.§ The tenement was then vaguely described as parcel of lands and possessions of a foundation in the church of All Saints, Barking Church, and if Stow's statement is correct, must have represented part of the actual site of the chapel. This conclusion is supported by the fact that when in that same year James Castelyn claimed that he had taken over Grace Smythe's lease, and

---

* *Ibid.*, 1536.
† J. Stow, *Survey of London* (ed. Kingsford), i, 131.
‡ *Ct. of Husting, Deeds Enr. R.* 267, No. 13 ; and *cf.* the ratebooks for the dates cited, in the church safe.
§ *Augm. Off., Particulars for Grants*, 1902 ; *cf. Church Deed*, 122. (11).

19

tried to recover occupation against John Haynnes and James Awood, one of the evidences put in was a copy* of the indulgence as it occurs in the register of the Bishop of London.

The petition, however, relates to "three messuages." It may therefore have referred not only to the two large buildings owned by the Wynters, but also to a very small house, separately rated at 2d. which was assessed in 1579 upon William Morris as tenant, and widow Archer owner. This small house apparently came at the corner of "Chappell Alley" where there dwelt only two paupers and a certain Robert Evers who paid 2d. in 1580. In fact, the arrangement of the rate-books here looks as though Evers had succeeded Morris. In any case this solitary allusion to "Chappell Alley" close to the Wynters' tenements again supports Stow's statement as to the site of the chapel.

The exact site of the chapel could only be determined by further research. We know from various deeds relating to tenements to the east and north-east of it, that it abutted northwards upon a considerable property which had been given to St. Paul's Cathedral by Master Thomas Northflete, one of the Canons, who endowed an obit in the Cathedral in 1317. From the very scanty deeds relating to Northflete's endowment,† we gather that some of his property lay in St. Olave's parish and that at least a part of it abutted westwards on the highway of Seething Lane. We know also that eastwards the chapel abutted on tenements in what was a northern extension of Chicken Lane, which was afterwards thrown into Tower Hill or "Roomland."‡ Robert Tate's instruction for his chantry chapel to be built out northwards only so far as ground could be spared shows that the Lady Chapel was on the extreme northern limits of the churchyard; but the ancient boundaries of the churchyard are difficult to define, and were probably irregular, for the Chicken Lane tenement abutting on the Chapel west abutted south on the churchyard. All the evidence, however, goes to support the considered and final conclusion of a former curate§ that the chapel lay in the cemetery some distance to the north of the church, on a site now pierced by the Underground Railway.

11.—*Medieval Worship in All Hallows*

Let us return to the church itself and try to catch a glimpse of the numerous services, matins, mass and evensong, the canonical hours and the frequent processions, in which the chantry chaplains and mass-priests took their part with the vicar and his deputy the parish priest.

* This copy is still in the church safe.
† *Penes* Dean and Chapter, St. Paul's, Box A. Deeds 527–31.
‡ *Husting R.*, 121, No. 153; 130, Nos. 91, 104; *cf.* Stow, *op. cit.* i. 130.
§ Maskell, *Berkingcherche* (2nd ed.) p. 9, cf. annotated copy of 1st ed. at B.M. 10358. i. 5; *cf.* Corner, *Sepulchral Memorials of All Hallows Barking* (Lond. and Middx. Arch. Soc., ii, 244).

20

THE PARISH OF ALL HALLOWS BARKING

The statutes of the Royal Chapel ordained that the chantry chaplains should on Sundays, Wednesdays and Fridays say the service for the dead, Lauds and Commendations according to the use of Sarum. This use superseded the old use of St. Paul's, London, in the cathedral church in 1414, and quickly made its way in the diocese. An inventory of All Hallows in 1452 apparently shows that this church was then adopting the new Sarum Use, for (in addition to new graduals and antiphoners) the church owned two old antiphonaries " of olde Salesbury use," and also two graduals " olde not Salesbery." Whence it may be inferred that the new books were of new Sarum Use, while some of the old ones were of old Sarum Use, and some not of Sarum Use at all but presumably of London Use.

There is little in the medieval inventories* of All Hallows' church goods to show how the vestments or hangings were used. In medieval times there was no hard and fast rule for colours in parish churches. The best and newest vestments and those with much gold or embroidery were used for great festivals, and faded ones for ordinary Sundays or weekdays with little regard for colour. Red was commonly used for martyrs, white for Our Lady and virgins, black for the dead. What was practically universal in England was the " Lenten array," viz. the covering of all pictures and images with white cloths marked with crosses, the instruments of the passion, and the like, and this was extended to the altar frontals and vestments which were also of similar white material. Usually red was substituted for the frontals and vestments in Passiontide and on Good Friday, the other white veils remaining. This was evidently the practice in All Hallows. St. Stephen's altar had frontal and curtains of white " steyned with the passion for lenten," and the high altar had in 1452 a vestment of white fustian " for lenten " and a *ferial* vestment of white russet rayed " for lenten," while in 1512 St. Anne's altar had a curtain of white " for the upper part " for Lent. The Lenten altar cloth in St. Nicholas' chapel had red crosses. There is record of a single vestment of red for Good Friday in 1452. The green bawdkin altar cloth with " All Hallowe " thereon which the church owned in 1506 may have been used for the patronal festival.

The hangings at the several altars were of red, white, green and " blue."† In 1452 there were for the high altar a " front and counterfront " of red satin‡ with frontal of red cloth of gold and curtains of red " tartaryn " given by John Pontrell; front, counterfront and frontal§ of white " tartaryn " powdered with " blue " garters with white curtains, which were given by John Croke; a frontal of green silk which went with front and

---

* Where no other reference is given, the following account is based upon the three inventories in the church safe, which are printed as appendices at pp. 70, *et seq.*

† Some authorities take this as the equivalent of purple.

‡ The " counterfront " was probably a dorsal of much the same size as the altar frontal here called the " front." F. E.

§ The " frontal " seems to be used for the frontlet, the narrow band of silk along the edge of the altar which hides the hooks for hanging the frontal and is often wrongly called the superfrontal nowadays. F. E.

counterfront of red cloth of gold; and a front and counterfront of blue . . . "stained" or painted with stars with two curtains "steyned with angels"; and there were also old frontals, including one of green, yellow and red. The Lady altar had a counterfront and curtains of green and white with a frontal of blue silk; the Trinity altar had cloths and curtains of white "steyned with briddes (or byrdes eyne) of gold"; St. Stephen's altar had cloths and curtains of white silk with garters, and others of white and green; and for the small altars in general there were frontals of several colours, blue stained with gold roses, green and red with gold flowers, white cloth of gold, another stained with the Apostles' heads, another stained with buckles of gold. There were curtains of green stained with angels and white roses, and others with a W crowned and a merchant's mark. These curtains in all cases probably hung close to each end of the altar on iron rods at right angles to the wall behind. In addition the choir was screened off by two other curtains being long "ridels" of blue.

By 1506 there had been added for the high altar the green cloths "for above and beneath" with All Hallows embroidered on the upper cloth, and also, for the altar of St. Nicholas black hangings, viz. a cloth of black worsted with a crucifix and the figures of Mary and John and with two curtains of black sarsenet. The Trinity altar then had a cloth depicting St. Katherine and St. Margaret with a silk frontal powdered with branches and curtains of "stained" linen. By 1512, the high altar also had a special cloth "of the trynyte," perhaps identical with the front of red cloth of gold embroidered with the Trinity previously given by Dame Margery Welton, and for St. Nicholas' altar there was a "cloyth steynyd with sent grygorys petty* with ij courtens of scheker sylke on[e] haelffe brent." St. Anne's altar then also had hangings of white sarsenet with garters, a cloth of white and green baudkin, and a cloth and frontal of "blue" baudkin with the curtain of white for the upper part for Lent.

Thus the church was full of colour, which was brought out by the steady gleam of the oil-lamp burning before the rood, and by the softer light of candles, shining at high mass through the smoke of incense which arose from the one censer of gilded copper, or from that other which had been beaten out of Dame Margery Haydok's silver girdle. The actual altar lights would not exceed two, set in the Galleymen's† silver candlesticks, or in the two standard candlesticks of latten standing before the high altar, or in the "middle candlesticks" for weddings. Other lights were set in the curtain rods, or in standards or hung from the roof. Six lesser latten candlesticks were used for more general purposes, and along the rood-loft thirty-one candles burned in thirty-one bowls of latten. At "morrow mass" there burned on the left or north side of the altar a single candle in a special candle-

---

* St. Gregory's pity, *i.e.* the "image of pity," viz. Our Lord rising from the tomb and displaying the sacred wounds as in His passion, appearing to St. Gregory as he was saying Mass. (See Henry Bradshaw Soc., XXII. *Ordinale Sarum sive Directorium Sacerdotum*, ed. Cooke and Wordsworth, London, 1902, ii, 646 *seq*.). F. E.

† See below, p. 30.

stick "with a nose," probably having a socket instead of the more usual spike to hold the candle. Many of the torches, which were stored in a long coffer before the Lady altar, were bequeathed by parishioners to burn at the Elevation after they had been used for the donors' funeral rites. Geoffrey Hughes, citizen and merchant-tailor of London and governor of the Tower under Henry VIII, ordained* that twelve new torches should burn about his body at *placebo* and *dirige* and mass and be borne by twelve poor honest men when he was buried before the rood in the body of the church, where his predecessor John Churche already lay. Four great new tapers, "of the biggest that may be gotten" were to be held about the hearse by four poor men. On the hearse itself were to stand two "braunches of virgin wax" which† were to be set afterwards upon the high altar at divine service there to burn before the Blessed Sacrament. Such lights gleamed on the best cross of wood plated with enamelled silver, weighing in all, with its figures of Mary and John, 62 ounces, or upon the Galleymen's gift, a wooden cross plated with silver and standing upon a copper foot. Both crosses, being of wood, probably came from Italy, the Galleymen's home.

A small silver pyx weighing six ounces hung under a canopy above the high altar. It was the gift of Dame Margery Welton,‡ who died in 1437, and also presented to the church the "resurrection" described below, a silver chrismatory for the holy oils and a good new missal. Besides Dame Margery Welton's pyx, the church owned a great standing pyx, or "coupe for the sacrement" weighing about 17 ounces. This was a covered cup with a cross and the figures of Mary and John, and was possibly that silver cup with a cover that Margery Haydok bequeathed in 1447.§ It was doubtless at the high altar that use was made of the new missal with clasps of silver and gilt which was given by the vicar Sir Nicholas Brymmesgrove, and of the great silver gilt chalice, weighing $51\frac{1}{2}$ ounces, and known as the "Knollis" chalice, which probably came from Sir Robert Knollys, an eminent general under the Black Prince and the preserver of Richard II from Wat Tyler's followers. He lived in Seething Lane and certainly gave to the church a suit of vestments of red cloth of gold. At the battle of Poitiers when he aided in the capture of the King of France and many of his nobles the following song‖ was sung of him:

Knollys

> *O Robert Knollis*
> *per te sit Francia mollis,*
> *Ense tuo tollis*
> *predas dans*
> *Vulnera collis.*

* *P.C.C.*, 4 Hogen.
† Or, more probably, the candles from which. F. E.
‡ Inventory, 1452. She seems to have given it in her lifetime, as it is not mentioned in her will. (*Comm. Lond.*, 482 More.) It may be that pyx which Virby's servant, William Walton, was charged with stealing. (*Mayor's Journ.* iii. 46, 47.)
§ *P.C.C.*, 116 Prowet.
‖ *Register of Bermondsey* (Harl. M.S. 231), f. 57.

There were nine chalices in all in 1452, eight of them marked with letters from A to H upon the patens; and the same number existed in 1512. Next to the Knollis chalice, the most remarkable were the two which were the gifts of the Galleymen, the chalice and paten weighing about 14 ounces "with the head of Jhesus thereupon," the seventeen-ounce parcel gilt chalice and paten given by Thomas Attemille and bearing "the arms of the whytte cross and a bar of gold going over," and a small chalice and paten of parcel gilt with a lamb thereon.

In addition to the covered cup, Margery Haydok gave a silver "halywaterstok" with a sprinkler (*isopo*), but in 1452 the church was still using holywaterstoups and sprinklers of latten. During the next sixty years, whilst the parishioners were doing much to enlarge and adorn their church, many additions were also made to its plate. The inventory of 1512 shows the addition of a silver-gilt monstrance, weighing nearly twelve pounds troy, for use in the Corpus Christi procession, and on Palm Sunday and Easter Day. Two silver paxes (for the kiss of peace) had also then been acquired, one with a crown and the other enamelled in blue. Two large silver basons, parcel gilt, one with a red cross (doubtless enamelled), and the other with red roses in the midst, and weighing together just under five pounds troy, were then in use, probably to decorate the altar when the plate was displayed, as was done on high days and is still done in one or two city churches and in Westminster Abbey and some other conservative foundations. A silver sanctus bell was also acquired by 1512, and the old pewter cruets for holding the wine and water for the Eucharist had been replaced by two silver cruets having a small cross upon them. Dame Margery Welton's hanging pyx had disappeared by 1512; perhaps it had been superseded by the "Round baylle [*sic*] of sylver and gylte for ye sacrament" which weighed 21 ounces.

The 15th century saw the provision of various additional services chiefly in connection with gilds and chantry foundations, and "pricksong," *i.e.* the more modern type of music began to develop. The inventory of church goods at All Hallows in 1452 includes, besides graduals, processionals and antiphoners, "one boke with ympnes noted" which by 1512 had been duplicated. It is interesting in passing to notice that the written church books of 1452 had by 1512 been supplemented with printed manuals and processionals. The enterprising vicar, Thomas Virby, when he died left to the church two surplices sleeved for the use of the choir. The Fraternity of Our Lady was anxious that its chaplains should be able both to chant and to sing when they took part in divine service within the church.* In 1486 Thomas Betson, stockfishmonger and merchant of the Staple of Calais, left 13s. 4d. yearly to pay for his obit, 6d. to every priest, 6d. to every clerk, 2d. to each child that sings every holyday in the same church, 20d. to the clerks for ringing the bells and 16d. to priests and clerks

---

* . . . in diebus dominicis et festiuis . . . ad diuini cultus augmentum eosdem capellanos in dicta ecclesia parochiali de Berking church . . . horis saltem canonicis maioreque misse per notam inibi decantand' et celebrand' cum cetteris psallentibus et psalmonizantibus volumus. (*Excheq. T. R., Misc. Bk.* 110.)

24

THE PARISH OF ALL HALLOWS BARKING

to " drink together where they list."* Betson's executor, Sir Robert Tate, left 20s. in 1500 to maintain " Our lady masse and Anteyn by note " in the Lady Chapel in the churchyard, and 6d. a week to a poor man to attend in the chapel and help the priest sing; he was also a patron of secular music and bequeathed £10 to the " mynstralls called the waytes of London in consideration of their grete labors and poure lyving."† Richard Fauconer, master-gunner to Henry VIII, desired in 1520, that the honest priest who was to sing for his soul, and that of his son Robert, should be a " queer-man."‡

In July 1519 there were already in the church a pair of organs with bellows " in the loft a bowff " and another pair of organs in the Lady Chapel when the Vicar, churchwardens and " Masters " of the parish called in Anthony Duddyngton citizen and organmaker to make them a new " in-strument, that is to say, a pair of organs for the church " at a total cost of £50. The specification§ for this work is of particular interest because of its early date. Duddyngton was to make:

" a pair of organs . . . of Dowble Cefaut viz., 27 playne kayes and the principall to contain the length of 5 foot so folowing with Bassys called Diapason to the same containing of length of 10 ft. or more. And to be Dowble pryncypalles thorowe out the seid Instrument so that the pyppes wᵗinforth shall be as fyne metall and stuff as the vtter partes that ys to say of pure Tyn with as fewe stoppes as may be convenient."

He was also to convey the bellows in the loft into the choir with a pipe to the " song bourde," and should the vicar and people not be content with the instrument when made, they were to allow him 40s. for his trouble in moving the bellows and he was to restore what was good‖ of the old instru-ment. When the new organs were duly installed, the churchwardens kept back part of the payment until they had been tested for a year, and Dudding-ton agreed to keep them, and the organs in the Lady Chapel, in order so long as he should live for a yearly fee of 6s. 8d.

Church music at this date seems to have been superseding the church drama. All Hallows still owned its properties for the Corpus Christi festival, but (as elsewhere), the pageant was falling out of use, and the church-wardens were concerned to find storage for the properties and to keep them in repair. They therefore let out to one John Scott¶ all their " pagantes . . . lonyng to [their] processys on corpus cristi day." Scott undertook to return them as they were at the end of 10 years, and to pay 10s. a year, abating the arrears of rent for the " standing." There was much to be done then to make them presentable; " it is not unknowe " (Scott says) " yt yei wyll cost me or yei be able to be occupyed xls and more." At another time

---

* *P.C.C.*, 24 Logge.
† App. VI.
‡ *P.C.C.*, 14 Maynwaryng.
§ *Church Deed*, No. 1.
‖ " the rest of the Truest."
¶ *Church Deed*, No. 6. (1).

D

(perhaps after the repairs had been completed) Scott hired* the "parcelles" for the Corpus Christi pageant at 13s. 4d. for little over a year, agreeing, however, to let the churchwardens have them on Corpus Christi day, or its Octave, or at any other season, and to restore them unbroken. The neighbouring Priory of Holy Trinity borrowed the properties of All Hallows for their Easter Resurrection pageant in 1515. The Cellarer of the Priory provided other "harness" for the "Resurrection," paid various waits and minstrels and gave 6s. 8d. to the keepers of Barkyng procession for the hire of their pageant against Easter.† The borrowed properties may have included a "Resurrection," the gift of Dame Margery Welton‡, which was doubtless a figure of Our Lord with a transparent jewel in the breast to show the host inside it, and is described among the church goods in 1452 as "a resurreccion of silver and ouergilt with a birell for the sacrament weying of troye weight iiij lb. vj unces," and in 1512 as "a Resurrection with a tombe a croysse and a scryne all syluer and gyllte" and weighing 53½ oz., the beryl then being separate and returned as weighing 3 oz. It was quite distinct from the great monstrance of silver and gilt and weighing 140½ oz. which the church acquired between 1452 and 1512.

The "resurrection" was used for the solemn ceremonies of Passion Week, when the host, consecrated on Maundy Thursday was set in the figure to show through the beryl, and veiled in one of the church's four "kerchiefs of pleasaunce" was "buried" in the tomb, or sepulchre, to the north of the high altar, until it was brought forth on Easter Day. All Hallows hung its sepulchre with "blue veluewet embrouded with sterres of gold of cipres," and set above it a kind of false sky or "celour steyned (i.e. painted) with the Trinitee." On Easter Day the parishioners all flocked to partake of the Sacrament which was administered to them across the "longe towell for houselyng on Esterday containing xiij elles large" (1452), so that no crumb should fall to the ground. At Easter also the church showed its joy by removing the veils, which since the beginning of Lent had hidden all its altars and images, the "veill of white lynnen cloth" (for the high altar) and seventeen "peces grete and smale for the auters and to hele the ymages in lenten tyme," the "cloth steyned with the passion," which covered the rood, and the "longe cloth steyned hangyng before the rode lofte." In December took place another drama, more riotous, when the Boy Bishop wore one of the "mitres for seynt Nicholas bisshop," choosing either the one with roses or the one with stars, and with his assistants donned the "two litell copes of grene for children" (1452) or the cope of white bawdekin for St. Nicholas powdered with garters with a gown and hood of red (1506), or the "four rockets for children" (1512). So through a series of pictures the church taught the illiterate people, who learned off by heart what they

---

* *Church Deed*, No. 6. (2).
† *L. & P., Hen. VIII*, ii (1) 115.
‡ It was given in her lifetime, for in her will her pious bequests relate only to a chaplain to sing for her soul and those of her three husbands and to the provision of 18 torches to burn about her body at burial (*Comm. Lond.*, 482 More).

THE PARISH OF ALL HALLOWS BARKING

might of the complex forms of worship, as did the four poor men who stood weekly on Saturdays in the Lady Chapel in the churchyard to earn an honest penny by saying for the soul of Robert Ingo the psalm *De profundis* or, if they could not manage so much, Our Lady's psalter.*

12.—*Chapels and Chantries*

Londoners have always made much of a funeral, and many of the medieval parishioners of All Hallows have left no record of themselves except directions for their burial and for prayer for their souls. Alderman John Croke, citizen and skinner, who lies below the altar tomb in the north-east chapel of the church, gave his houses in London, Middlesex and Calais to his wife, and afterwards to the church, on condition they should maintain a chantry chaplain at the altar of St. Nicholas for himself, his parents and friends, and should maintain an obit to be sung (*per notam*) yearly by the vicar, chaplains and clerks on the anniversary of his death, with *placebo* and *dirige* on the eve and requiem mass on the morrow, and with the tolling of bells and all observances meet for such an obit such as are kept in the city of London (1477)†. A special fee was given for burial in the chancel, thus Sir William Hawkes, probably a chaplain, who was buried in the chancel, gave to " Maister Vicar for Mortuary after the custom of this noble city my best gown, and for the place of my sepulture my best surplice."‡ A general bede-roll for the dead was read weekly at mass on Sundays. John Pakyn, citizen and shipwright, gave 20s. to the church repairs in 1483 to be prayed for in this bede-roll among other persons.§ Simon, or " Symkyn " Hugh, citizen and cloth-worker, in 1410 left a whole new vestment of black and green for perpetual prayer for his soul, while the vestment should last, " so that the vicar or parish chaplain should commend my soul for prayer every Sunday among others by name." ‖ This suit headed the list of vestments in 1452, and appears in the inventory of 1506 as " two old copys of blake wythe brawnchys of grene sylke wythe prest deken and subdeken," so that Symkyn's gift ensured a century of remembrance in his parish church. About 1521 the celebration of Morrow Mass, said very early in the morning, had been begun in this church, and John Kervyle, mercer, then left 1s. a year for twenty years for " its good continuance if it be kept as it is now begun."¶ But many parishioners made more definite provision for masses and prayers for their souls after death, and this custom increased among them in the 15th century with the growing insistence upon the doctrine of purgatory, ceasing only towards the end of Henry VIII's reign, as the authority of the State enforced the doctrines of the Reformation. With some poor souls, the fear of purgatory evidently approached to panic. Simon Hugh, in addition to

Croke

* *P.C.C.*, 15 Moone.
† App. V.
‡ *P.C.C.*, 16 Fetiplace.
§ *Comm. Lond.*, 342 Wilde.
‖ *Ibid.*, 174 Broun.
¶ *P.C.C.*, 3 Ayloffe.

27

the other pious provisions in his will, gave instructions shortly before his death in 1410 for a chaplain to celebrate in All Hallows church and in the Lady Chapel near (i.e. in the churchyard) for seven years, celebrating in the first year a trental (thirty masses) of St. Gregory, and also exhorted his executors to have three thousand masses celebrated for his soul with all haste after his death. Blanche Medford, who wished to be buried nigh the altar of St. Anne, beside John Bolle, one of her three husbands, asked in 1493 that one hundred masses " should be done for her soul as soon as may be."* Roger Hewett, tailor, not longe before his death in 1534, ordained that there should be sung for his soul immediately after his death five masses of the Wounds of Our Lord, five masses in honour of the Passion, and five masses in honour of the name of Jesu, and that there should be said three masses in honour of our Blessed Lady " to thentent that she may praye and bee meane (i.e. mediator) to her swete sonne Jesu for my soule, for my father and mother soules," also seven masses of the Assumption of Our Lady, and three in honour of the sorrows that she suffered at the Passion.†

Tonge

The earliest record we have of such provisions is the will of Cecily le Mulvard who in 1286 desired a trental (*i.e.* thirty masses) in " Berking-church " for the good of her soul.‡ A century later there were several chaplains in the church, for Richard Amuresden, himself one of them, left 20d. in 1385 to every chaplain celebrating continually there.§ William de Tonge, a citizen of London, who in 1389 left 10 marks to purchase a legend‖ for the use of the parishioners, ordered that three of the best chaplains should celebrate in All Hallows church for five years after his death for his soul and the souls of his parents, stipulating that they should be present at all the canonical hours, viz. matins, mass and evensong, at a yearly salary of ten marks (£6 13s. 4d.).¶ There are many 15th-century bequests for a priest " of good and honest conversation," or a " virtuous priest and a good quire-man " to celebrate for a year or two in the church for the testators' souls. The chaplain's salary usually came out of the estate, sometimes from property earmarked for the purpose. John Rolff, shipwright, gave instructions in 1432 that his wharf in " Petit Wales " should be sold to provide a chaplain in All Hallows for two years,** and Richard Colyn, a linen draper, buried in 1452 before the rood in the chapel of St. Stephen's, having had difficulty in recovering a debt of £21 from a Dartmouth merchant, desired his executors, if they could get it in, to use it for a chaplain who should celebrate for a year before the image of the Virgin Mary in the church.†† Joan Mortilman, whose husband's account for repairs to the old parish houses and the church remained unpaid in 1505, upon his death forgave the church her portion

* *P.C.C.*, 8 Vox.
† *Comm. Lond.*, 235 Tunstall.
‡ Sharpe, *Cal. of Husting Wills*, i, 177.
§ *Comm. Lond.*, 129 Courtney.
‖ Probably a book containing the lessons, rather than a copy of the *Legenda aurea*. F. E.
¶ *P.C.C.*, 2 Rous.
** *Comm. Lond.*, 349 More.
†† *Ibid.*, 56 Sharp.

of the debt, and also agreed " to do and say for the best to " her son-in-law to forgive the other portion, so that the " parische and the paryssons maye the better have the sowll of my seyd husband in ther remembranz."*

Members of the City Companies would strive by gifts to the Company to make sure of many prayers at their funerals or the yearly obit afterwards. For instance, Nicholas Jenyn, a wealthy skinner who had his dwelling " place " in the parish, and houses and a " key " in Petit Wales, bequeathed to the Skinners' Company a house called the Ram's Head in Eastcheap in 1531, on condition they kept a yearly obit for him in All Hallows church, spending thereon 40s., which included payments to the Company's officers and 4d. each for those of the company who attended, besides five shillings' worth of bread and ale for the wardens, priests and clerk.†

Devotional guilds for the common maintenance of a chaplain to celebrate for the well-being of the living members and for the souls of the dead probably existed in the church in number greater than that recorded. None of these, however, was of so great an importance as the Fraternity of Our Lady, which governed the royal chantry chapel in the churchyard. We have record only of one other brotherhood, namely that of St. Anne. The church owned " two quaieres of the story of seint Anne " in 1452. The chapel of St. Anne was next that of St. Stephen, before the rood. In the latter half of the 15th century it became a burial place for the Colyn family. Richard, Colyn, linen-draper, desired in 1451 to be buried in the chapel of St. Stephen‡, but his widow Rose and son John both prayed to be buried " next " him, in the chapel of St. Anne§. In November 1471 William Thomson, mariner, wished to be buried before the image of St. Anne, bequeathing to the church repairs his " best white harneys " and to him that should " go for me in pilgrimage to St. Romyon " 20s.|| Thomson's wife died in childbed a month after her husband and was buried beside him, leaving to the church repairs her " best coverlet of arras work " and to the new-born child her best gown of blue furred grey and her husband's two whistles¶. Margaret Henham, widow, in April 1505 when she was about to attempt the " casuall and jeopardous " passage overseas to Calais, where her husband lay buried, desired if she died in London to be buried before this altar of St. Anne**; John Pownson, a Breton mariner, bequeathed 8d. to St. Anne in Barking church where his wife and child already lay in 1515††. The earliest known reference to a guild of St. Anne dates, however, from 1520 when Richard Fauconer gave 3s. 4d. to the brotherhood of St. Anne‡‡;

---

* *Church Deed*, 34.
† *P.C.C.*, 22 Thower.
‡ *Comm. Lond.*, 56 Sharp.
§ *Ibid.*, 331, 370 Sharp; *cf.* below, p. 31.
|| *Ibid.*, 93 Wilde.
¶ *Ibid.*
** *P.C.C.*, 6 Adeane.
†† *Comm. Lond.*, 106 Bennet.
‡‡ *P.C.C.*, 14 Maynwaring.

while in 1527 Bartholomew Worrall, a parishioner and greytawyer, bequeathed 20s. to "the brotherhood of St. Anne kept in the said church [of All Hallows] to pray for me."* Three altar cloths were set apart for St. Anne's altar in 1512, and to these John Fyssher in 1517 added a pair of sheets,† probably to cut up, or for use as dust-sheets.

The "Galymen," or Italian merchants who lived in Mincing Lane and brought their wares ashore at "Galley Key" in Petit Wales, just south of All Hallows, clubbed together to make gifts to the church; but no record has been found of any guild among them to maintain a priest there. Their gifts as recorded in the inventory of 1452 were two silver candlesticks, weighing 1 lb. 2¾ oz.; a [wooden] cross plated with silver‡ with a copper foot weighing with the "tree" (or wood) 4 lb. 8 oz. troy, two chalices, and a new banner of white "tartaryn" with an image (or picture) of Our Lady.

There was great building activity during the latter part of the 15th century.§ It was then that the chancel arcades were rebuilt, the chancel arch removed and a new clerestory built in the nave as a continuation of the new one in the chancel. The chancel aisles were also extended to their present length on a line with the east wall. It is possible also that the whole of the aisles were widened at this date.

Such evidences as remain show that the rood screen and loft, to which large bequests were then being made, were exceptionally important features of the church. The rood seems to have extended across both aisles, as is indicated by the wider spacing of the eastern arches of the nave arcade and the irregular position of the windows. This rood was reconstructed during the latter half of the 15th century. Before it in 1377 had stood the chapel of St. Stephen, for Joan, the widow of Thomas Snetesham, then desired to be buried beside her husband in the chapel of St. Stephen before

---

* *Comm. Lond.*, 149 Tunstall.

† *Ibid.*, 42 Bennet.

‡ This may well have been brought from their own country, Italy, where the wooden cross plated with silver was a common type. F. E.

§ *See* the wills of Simon Hugh, 1410, £40 to rebuild the church roof (*Comm. Lond.*, 174 Broun); Nicholas Bene, 1400, works of the church 40d. (*Comm. Lond.*, 468 Courtney); John Rolff, 1432, 10 marks to the church fabric (*Comm. Lond.*, 349 More); John Cok, 1440, 20s. to fabric of church and £5 to the fabric of "le yle" of the same church if begun within 2 years (*Comm. Lond.*, 44 Prowet); Richard Colyn, 1451, 5 marks to church works (*Comm. Lond.*, 56 Sharp); Sibyl Salveyn, 1453, 6s. 8d. for church works (*Comm. Lond.*, 111 Sharp); Aleyn Johnson, 1457, 20s. for church works (*Comm. Lond.*, 222 Sharp); John Dobbes, clerk, 1457, 3s. 4d. for new work of the church (*Comm. Lond.*, 217 Sharp); John Baker, 1456, to the fabric of the body of the church £40 to be expended where most necessary (*P.C.C.*, 10 Godyn); Lawrence Coke, 1466, 20d. to the church work (*Comm. Lond.*, 393 Sharp); Thomas à Wode, 13s. 4d. to church works, 1468 (*Comm. Lond.*, 36 Wilde); John Croke, 1477, £40 to works and building of the church, £40 to the rood (*P.C.C.*, 33 Wattys); Elizabeth Johnson, 1481, 20s. to church works (*Comm. Lond.*, 369 Wilde); Thomas Breton, 1483, reparation of roodloft 40 marks (*P.C.C.*, 24 Logge); Thomas Gilbert, 1484, to church works as most necessary (*P.C.C.*, 21 Logge); John Evyngar, 1496, painting and setting up of rood, 26s. 8d. (*P.C.C.*, 2 Horne); Thomas Stodard, 1496, church works, 40s. (*Comm. Lond.*, 119 Harvy); and one of the church deeds (No. 34) dated 1505, whereby Joan Mortylman forgives the church a debt due to her late husband for reparations done to the church.

the cross.* Others who were buried in St. Stephen's chapel were William Tilling, chaplain, who left a black worsted vestment to the chapel in 1430, Richard Colyn in 1451, and John Lovell in 1470†. The position of the chapel is further indicated by the will of Sir John Vale " chaplain of the chantry " in All Hallows church who wished to be buried before the high altar under the stone of Sir William Tylling, formerly chaplain of the said chantry. The only perpetual chantry then existing within the church was that of Thomas Pilkes, founded in 1348, and it seems possible that his chantry chapel was at the altar dedicated to St. Stephen. There are references to the altar of St. Stephen in the inventory of 1452, but not later. The chapel must have been a little to one side, just before the rood; next it came the chapel of St. Anne, for John Colyn in 1462, and Rose Colyn in 1465, desired to be buried in the chapel of St. Anne next to the Richard Colyn, who had been buried in St. Stephen's chapel in 1451‡.

The third chapel of which the position can be inferred was that of St. Nicholas. John Croke, whose tomb still exists on the north side of the north chancel aisle, endowed a chantry at the altar of St. Nicholas in 1477.§ It may therefore be concluded that St. Nicholas' altar was in the north aisle. A parish where watermen, mariners and shipwrights abounded was almost certain to do honour to the patron saint of sailors. We have seen how the parishioners prepared for the festivities of the Boy Bishop, and it is certain that as early as 1310 there was an altar of St. Nicholas in the church, as Peter Blakeney then desired to be buried near it and bequeathed 13s. 4d. for the pavement before it.|| The altar was possibly removed eastwards when this aisle was extended, or a smaller chapel of St. Nicholas may have already stood to the north of the chancel.¶ Robert White, a brewer, was buried in the chapel of St. Nicholas in 1495, and Thomas Stodard, a woodmonger, in 1496; and there are references to the altar in the inventory of 1512.

Two other altars have not as yet been located. The one dedicated to the Holy Trinity is mentioned both in the inventory of 1452 and in that of 1512. The other had a double dedication to Our Lady and St. Thomas (so in the inventory of 1512), but was usually styled the altar of Our Lady. That it was quite distinct from the free Lady Chapel within the churchyard is shown by the inventories of 1452 and 1512, and by the will of Richard Colyn desiring that a chaplain should celebrate before the image of the Virgin in the church.

Only two perpetual chantry chapels existed in the church when Edward VI suppressed all chantries in 1548. The one was that established by Thomas Pilkes, citizen of London, who was buried in the churchyard

* *Comm. Lond.*, 50 Courtney.
† *Ibid.*, 243 More, 62 Wilde.
‡ *Ibid.*, 56 Sharp; *cf.* above, p. 29.
§ See pp. 27, 32.
|| See below, p. 32.
¶ See Architectural Description, p. 54.

near to the Lady Chapel. By his will,* dated 1349, he gave all his lands, rents and tenements within the parish to his mother for her life, then to his wife for her life, and after that to maintain a chaplain in All Hallows church. The rector and four of the most honest and able parishioners were to see that the chaplain conducted himself well and honestly in divine service and in keeping the houses in repair. He was to be present constantly at mass, matins, vespers, and all canonical hours and every night or day was to say *placebo* and *dirige* with commendation for the souls of the founder, his mother and wife, and his wife's daughter Ellen. The presentation to the chantry was in the Bishop of London, but the chaplains found it necessary from time to time to get royal confirmation, as when Robert Hykedy, the chaplain who had been duly presented, secured from Richard II in 1387 confirmation of his estate " in consideration of the pious purpose of [the founder] and the long usage and custom of the City of London."† There is no indication as to the particular altar in the church at which Pilkes' chaplain celebrated; but for the reasons set out above, it seems very likely that it was in the chapel of St. Stephen.

The second chantry was founded in 1477‡ by a wealthy skinner, Alderman John Croke, who lived in Mark Lane. His widow Margaret, so long as she lived, was to find a chaplain to celebrate for him at the altar of St. Nicholas. After her death, his Mark Lane house with other tenements went to the Vicar and Wardens of All Hallows, who were bound to use the profits for keeping his anniversary, and for the maintenance of a perpetual chaplain at the altar of St. Nicholas.

The Blakeney family had tried in vain to establish a perpetual chantry at that altar. Adam Blakeney in 1295 charged land and a wharf in the parish to maintain a chaplain. Peter Blakeney, a citizen of London who lived on the east side of Mark Lane, left for the maintenance of a chantry priest at the altar of St. Nicholas a tenement called Blakelofte on the west of Mark Lane, and another on the east of the lane, in St. Olave's parish just north of his own home; but his executors omitted to obtain a licence from the King for thus making an alienation in mortmain, and eventually Edward III seized the two tenements in Mark Lane and gave them to the Abbey of St. Mary Graces near the Tower, which was of his own foundation. Meantime John of Cambridge (Grauntebregg), apparently a connection of Blakeney's, about 1329 charged his own dwelling house in Mark Lane to maintain a chantry in All Hallows for the good of the souls of Peter Blakeney, and Blakeney's wife Cecily, Alice his own dead wife, his son John and others. His executors and their heirs were to call in three or four of the best and lawful men of the parish to help them appoint a chaplain; but the house was so much out of repair when John of Cambridge died, that the executors, with the alderman of the ward and several parishioners, were fain to let it at once to one Godwin Turke, fishmonger, who, following the example of John of

* *Husting R.*, 78, No. 251.
† *Cal. Patent Rolls*, 1385–89, p. 360.
‡ See App. V; *cf.* pp. 27, 31 above.

THE PARISH OF ALL HALLOWS BARKING

Cambridge, agreed to maintain the chaplain, either from the profits of the house in Mark Lane or—should it be destroyed by fire or go to ruin—from his own tenement in Spurier (now Water) Lane. In 1350 Godwin Turke's widow, Parnel, gave the tenement in Mark Lane, which by then included a brewery, to the rector and parishioners; but even these arrangements failed to secure permanency for the chantry, and in 1392 Bishop Braybroke agreed that the endowments of Adam Blakeney and John of Cambridge should be united for the maintenance of a chaplain to celebrate for ever for the souls of the founders, of all the faithful deceased, and all persons buried in All Hallows church. Still the chantry did not flourish, and no priest was celebrating for this foundation, when the Croke and Pilkes chantries were suppressed in 1548.*

The chantry priests were generally bound to take part in the usual services of the church, and these chaplains, permanent or temporary, must have augmented the choir throughout the Middle Ages. The Vicar was not always in residence, as Virby was; and he was often aided, or represented, by a parish priest or chaplain, such as "Sir† Stephen" the "parish chaplain" remembered in a shipwright's will in 1385, or "Nicholas" (probably Brymesgrove) the parish priest who received 12d. from William Godyng in 1400. Geoffrey Burgyn, citizen and vestmentmaker, had probably had business dealings with the "vicary," the parish priest, the chantry priest and the two clerks, to all of whom he made bequests for prayers in 1463, carefully grading his gifts according to the recipient's status, 12d. to the vicar, 6d. each to the two priests and 4d. to the clerks. The parish priest had disappeared by 1547, when it was returned that the vicar provided none.

Priest or vicar often bequeathed to the church his own books or vestments. Thus Sir Thomas Virby left, besides surplices, a manual with a collectar (i.e. a book of collects), and Sir Nicholas Brymmesgrove, who was vicar from 1403 onwards, gave the best missal with clasps of silver and gilt. The chantry chaplain, Sir William Tilling, bequeathed to All Hallows in 1430 his own red vestment of cloth of gold, which appears in the inventory of 1452 as a "single vestment of old cloth of gold red." The church then had many such single vestments and four complete "suits" of vestments for priest, deacon and subdeacon, such as the red cloth of gold suit given by Sir Robert Knolles, which included a chasuble, two tunicles, three albs, three amices, with the stoles and fanons (i.e. maniples) and a cope. By 1512, the church had nine different suits as well as single vestments. There was great variety of colour and texture in these medieval vestments. They ranged from the plain black worsted given by Sir William Tilling, chantry-priest, through the tawny damask with coneys and hounds on its orfreys, to purple bawdkin (a rich brocade) ornamented with roses and blue cranes. There was a red and green vestment adorned with lions of gold, another of blue velvet with white roses, and a third of white damask with branches‡ of gold. For Good

---

* For the wills in question see *Husting R.*, 24 (100), 40 (26), 57 (149).

† "Sir," here, is a courtesy title.

‡ "Branches" in this connection were probably narrow orphreys forming a Ψ on the chasuble. F. E.

33

Friday there was a single vestment of red. The donors besprinkled their gifts with initials : so we have in 1512 two copes of white damask with " Jes and Kays " (elsewhere " Js and Cayes ") of gold and orfreys of red cloth of gold. In 1506 blue silk bustian was " powdered " with " Esses and beasts " (perhaps for St. Stephen), white bustian with garters, white bawdkin with birds, and red bawdkin with crowns and beasts, while an old red cope (possibly William Tilling's) was powdered with beasts of gold.

The two clerks figure in many a parishioner's will as the master clerk and under clerk, or upper, and under clerk. It is curious to note that the clerk's wages at the time of the Elizabethan settlement, and possibly earlier, consisted of the pewrents, a variable total made up of small sums ranging from 2d. to 8s.; and this method of payment remained in force as late as 1670, when (owing to arrears) the Vestry made a new book of rates for the " clerk's wages or pewmoney " and meantime paid Mr. Richardson, then parish clerk, £10 on account. The clerks had the custody of the goods and ornaments belonging to the church, undertaking " sykerly and saffely to kepe [them] w[ith]in the same chyrche to the usse and proffet there of " during the term of their service, and to pay reasonably for anything that might be " aliened " or lost through their fault. To this end, in 1512, they each found good sureties in two good citizens of London. The sexton's main duty during the Middle Ages was the care of the many candles and lights in the church. One account of his in the early 16th century answers for numerous small payments including 16d. for Mr. Croke's obit, 5d. for five tapers on " alhalon day," two links weighing 6 lbs. on 11 December, and two tapers, half a pound, " on cheldermas," two tapers of half a pound at Easter with a roll of wax of another half-pound, possibly for the Paschal light. This light was apparently supplemented in All Hallows church by the ostrich feathers peculiar to London, for the inventory of 1452 includes twelve " pensels of Ostritch feders."

13.—*The Great Change*

All Hallows church had an intimate and tragic connexion with the beginnings of the Reformation in England. One of the earliest of those who suffered death for conscience' sake was the aged bishop John Fisher, who was executed on Tower Hill, 22 July, 1535, for refusing to acknowledge Henry VIII as Supreme Head of the Church in England. His headless body was buried without ceremony " in the churchyerd of Barkyne by the northe dore "; a few days later Sir Thomas More was beheaded for the same offence. " Then was tane up the byshoppe agayne and both of them burryd within the tower."*

The chronicler who thus recorded these events continued : " that same yere beganne the new testament in Englych." The reading of the Bible in the vernacular, and dependence upon the Bible as a supreme source of theo-

* *Chronicle of the Grey Friars of London* (Camden Soc.), 38.

THE PARISH OF ALL HALLOWS BARKING

logical truth, were essential parts of the Reformation in the English church as laid down by Henry VIII in 1536; yet William Tyndale, whose translation of the Bible has formed the basis of subsequent English versions, was in that very year an exile for his Zwinglian opinions, and later suffered martyrdom in the Low Countries. In 1537 there was buried in All Hallows churchyard one of Tyndale's former patrons, Alderman Humphrey Monmouth, who had taken a " fantasy " to the young scholar, but in 1528, finding himself in the Tower on suspicion of bringing heretical books from overseas, had asked whether he were to blame, if the chaplains and scholars whom he aided " turned as this priest had done." Monmouth was a draper trading overseas in Suffolk cloths, and had spread some of Tyndale's works, giving one to the abbess of Denny, getting another for a Greenwich friar, and " having no thought that they were not good," until the bishop of London preached at St. Paul's Cross and said that Tyndale had translated the New Testament " naughtily."* Monmouth's will,† however, proves his continued adherence to the reformers. He ordained that his burial should be without the ringing of bells or singing of dirges, and appointed as his executor Dr. Robert Barnes, who had been in exile for spreading the New Testament in England, until Thomas Cromwell had recalled him to support the doctrine of the royal supremacy. " Four godly ministers, Mr. Latimer, Dr. Barnes, Dr. Crome and Mr. Taylor " were to preach in Barking church four sermons a week till thirty sermons should be preached, in memory of Monmouth— instead of the former custom of providing thirty masses for the soul. The parishioners of All Hallows thus heard the reformed doctrines from some of their most notable exponents.

Monmouth

There is little record of the reception of the new opinions in the parish. In one or two earlier wills there are traces of reaction against extravagances, which had grown up around the doctrine of purgatory. For instance, Thomas Gilbert, a draper and merchant of the Staple of Calais, had in 1484 desired to be buried in the church and that his obit and mass should " not be done outrageously contrary to all reason for pomp and pride of this world . . . but to the laude and praysing of almightie god and to the helthe and comforte of my soule."‡ Whether from conviction, or from fear of the royal authority, the parishioners of All Hallows certainly ceased from about 1539 onwards to make in their wills those provisions for masses and prayers for the soul which accompany practically all their earlier bequests. The King's power was impressed upon them in 1546, when Henry, then on his deathbed, secured the execution of the soldier-poet, Earl of Surrey, whose kinship to the royal house threatened the royal plans for the succession. Surrey was beheaded on Tower Hill on the 19th of January, 1547, and his body rested in All Hallows churchyard until it was removed to his ancestral home at Framlingham in 1614.§

* *Letters & Papers Hen. VIII*, iv. 4282.
† *P.C.C.*, 12 Dyngeley.
‡ *Ibid.*, 21 Logge.
§ *Dict. Nat. Biog.*

THE PARISH OF ALL HALLOWS BARKING

With the death of Henry VIII came the triumph of the more advanced party of the Reformation, who were responsible for sweeping away the chantries, images and other "superstitious" ornaments and uses. It has been seen how the royal chapel in the churchyard perished in 1547. A like fate fell upon the chantries within the church. Then were ousted the two chantry priests, John Rudde, a man of good learning who was drawing a salary of £27 odd from the lands of Thomas Pilkes, for whose soul he celebrated, and John Batman, a priest who sang for the soul of John Croke in the chapel of St. Nicholas, at a yearly wage of £7; and the yearly obits for Croke and for William Kyrfote came to an end. The royal commissioners not only seized the whole of these endowments, including those profits which went to the poor, but also the tenement in Seething Lane which Isabel Hurar had given in 1348* to the fabric of the church, and the parish houses also in Seething Lane, which had come to the church from an unknown donor.†

The Vicar, William Dawes, presented in 1542, was left to carry on his work single-handed in a parish which was one of the very few city parishes numbering as many as 800 "houseling" people (*i.e.* communicants). He continued here through the various changes of the following years until his death in 1565, taking for his services £132 odd a year, and serving also the livings of Woodham Walter and Rivenhall in Essex. Thomas Pilkes' tenement, which was in Tower Street next the house and garden of his priest, John Rudd, had been let to one Nicholas Michell, a citizen and beerbrewer, for 66 years from 1st October, 1546, on which day Michell had also obtained a ninety-nine years' lease of the thirteen other tenements belonging to Pilkes' chantry and lying "upon the highway to the Towre Watergate." In May 1548, backed by John Yelde, a citizen and woodmonger, Michell bought all this property outright at eighteen years' purchase. An important part of the endowment of John Croke's chantry, viz. the great house in Mark Lane, which was occupied by William Denham on a fifty-three years' lease dating from 1541, together with two adjacent tenements and "shops cellars solars vaults and warehouses," was bought by Thomas Mildmay of Moulsham in Essex at fifteen years' purchase. The tenement called the "Sopehouse" in the parish, which was parish property, was sold at fourteen years' purchase to Thomas Reve and George Cotton in 1552.‡

Nicholas Michell, the brewer, was apparently an active supporter of the Edwardian church policy, and as churchwarden with John Hancockes in 1547 sold the church plate, which has been described above,§ for £77 odd, a sum as great as any made in that year by similar sales in London, expending £37 out of the proceeds "about the reparations of the church." Just before these changes, in 1546 there died William Thynne, who had been Master of the Household to Henry VIII, and in editing the works of

---

* Sharpe, *Cal. Husting Wills*, i. 532
† *Augm. Off.*, Chantry Cert. 34 (46).
‡ *Ibid.*, Partrs. for Grants, 2114, 1780, 1899.
§ See pp. 23, 24.

36

THE PARISH OF ALL HALLOWS BARKING

Thynne

Geoffrey Chaucer had included certain spurious tales attacking the medieval church. The brass to Thynne lies in the south-east aisle of the church, and both the terms of its inscription and the preamble to his will* breathe the new spirit of the Reformation.

The church records contain no indication of the effects of the Marian policy here. Philip Dennys, whose arms in brass remain upon the east wall of the north aisle, was buried in the church with something of the old ceremony in 1556. " The vj day of September was bered at Barking church in London master Phelype Dennys sqwyre, with cote [armour . . .] of armes, and ij whytt branchys and xij torchys, [iiij] grett tapurs, a ij dosen of skchochyons of armes; the wyche he was a goodly man of armes and [a great] juster."† The pluralist vicar, William Dawes, was then aided at All Hallows by a curate, Mr. Daniel, whom Dennys styled his " Ghostly Father." Of the Reformers who had preached Monmouth's memorial sermons in the church, Dr. Barnes had been burned at Smithfield in 1540, Dr. Crome saved his life, but not his liberty, by recanting in 1555, Bishop Latimer suffered martyrdom at Oxford that year and Bishop Taylor had forfeited his bishopric. And again the parishioners were eye-witnesses of the calamities which befell those who opposed Tudor authority. Lord Thomas Grey, whom ambition rather than any religious motive had involved in the rebellion of Sir Thomas Wyatt, was on 28th April, 1554, " heddyd on Towre hyll, betwyn IX and X of the cloke a-for none . . . and bered at Allalow's Barkyng."‡ In July 1556 Henry Peck-ham and John Danyell, conspirators who hoped to help seize the Exchequer and depose Philip and Mary in favour of Elizabeth, were hanged on the gallows on Tower Hill and afterwards beheaded, and their heads set upon London Bridge; but their bodies were buried in All Hallows church.§

It is possible that the injunctions of the Edwardian reformers had not been completely executed in the church, for the rood still remained in 1558, unless it had been restored during the reign of Mary. Apparently the five altars of St. Nicholas, Our Lady and St. Thomas, the Trinity, St. Anne and St. Stephen had been destroyed by the Edwardian reformers, and under Queen Mary two side altars only had been replaced.

Immediately after Elizabeth's accession, the rood was taken down, the side altars removed and the high altar replaced by a communion table. The churchwardens' account for 1559‖ records these changes as follows :

---

* " Firste I bequeathe my soul to my swete Saviour through Christ my only Redeemer, and to the whole holly companie of Heven, of which in faithe I believe to be one of them through the merytes of Christ's passion and no otherwise." (*P.C.C.*, 17 Alen, cited by Maskell, Berkynge-chirche (1864) 54).

† *Diary of Henry Machyn* (Camden Soc.), 113.

‡ *Ibid.*, 61.

§ *Ibid.*, 109; *Cal. S. P. Dom.*, 1547–80, pp. 81–84.

‖ Among the church records. The account is undated, but a comparison of the entries for burial fees with the register shows that it belongs to the year from Easter 1559 to Easter 1560.

Receipts]. Item solde the beame of the Roodelofte at 4d. the
fote, 12 fote and a half a mounting to the some of   4s.   2d.
     Item solde 5 smale peces of tymber that laye at the steppes
of the alter at 3½d the foote mounting to 9 fote and a half some is   2s.   1od.
     Item solde the 2 syde alter stones to Mr Fyssher   1os.
     Item solde the stone of the highe alter to Thomas Garret
and Nicholas Awgoure for   6s.   8d.

[Paid].
     Item to a Carpenter for takinge downe of the Crucyfix, the
Marye and John and alhallowes the patrone   2od.
     To a workman for 3 daies worke for takinge down the alters 3s. 6d.
     To 4 laborers for 3 daies worke at 1od. the daie   1os.
     For the carying a waie of 6 lodes of rubbyshe   3s.
     For a workeman to poole downe the Beame in the Rowdelofte
and other thinges that was to do in the churche for twoo daies   2s. 4d.
     For wasshinge the churche walles where the alters stode and
2 dosens of Spanish white at 8d. the dossen   16d.

This same account includes, also, the payments for setting up the
Communion Table and buying the new service books.

[Payments]
     Item for a Communion booke   2s. 8d.
     Item for a Communion table   11s. 2d.
     Item for a Service booke   5s. 4d.
     Item for the booke of Iniunctions and articles   4d.
     Item for putting upp the bill of articles   4d.
     Item for other chardges at dynner at the putting in the said
bill of articles   4s.
     Item for the booke called the Homilie   16d.

In the year ending with Lady Day, 1574, the churchwardens bought
the second " tome " of the Homilies and also the Homilies against rebellion
for 2s. This account shows us that both morning and evening prayer were
read by candle-light, and that the vicar, Richard Tyrwhit, who had succeeded
William Dawes in 1565, was aided by a curate, Mr. Phillips. The churchwardens allowed Mr. Phillips 6s. 8d. a quarter for reading morning
prayer. A hassock is also provided that year for the " lower pulpit." In
1580 the curate was receiving yearly 26s. 8d. Four new prayer-books were
bought for the church in that year, and considerable sums were expended
upon the making of the churchyard wall, repairs to the church doors and the
paving of the " lane." The curate then was probably John Tailor, who had
made answer to the visitation articles of Bishop Aylmer in 1579, reporting
that divine service was said and the sacraments administered according to the
Book of Common Prayer, except that the minister did not dip nor use the

sign of the cross in baptism. He did not intermeddle in affairs of state in preaching, nor did any unlicensed persons preach in the parish. No private fasts were kept, and so far as was known no conventicles existed in the parish, nor did any vagrant ministers dwell there without sufficient livelihood. Thus we gather, that the reply to Aylmer's inquiries as to complete acceptance of the Elizabethan settlement in this parish was that all was well, save in regard to the forms of baptism.*

The vicar, Richard Tyrwhit, died in 1585 and Archbishop Whitgift presented a chaplain of his own, Richard Wood, who aided Whitgift by his answers to the Marprelate Tracts and resigned about 1591. He was succeeded by Thomas Ravis, also a zealous conformist, who afterwards became Bishop of Gloucester and of London. In 1604 he was appointed to translate a part of the New Testament for the Authorised Version of the Bible, a work with which All Hallows church had an honourable and close connection, for Dr. Robert Tighe, who was vicar of All Hallows from 1598 until 1616, was also employed in this translation, by reason of his excellence as a textuary and linguist. More notable still is the birth in the parish of the learned Bishop Lancelot Andrewes, whose name stands first upon the list of translators.

During Elizabeth's reign the church received into its keeping men of diverse shades of opinion. Here was buried in 1560 William Armar, citizen and clothworker, who had succeeded in retaining office in the royal household through the reigns of Henry, Edward, Mary and Elizabeth, and whose brass with the motto " Lyve to Dye is ye Way to Life " remains upon a pillar in the south aisle. Here also was buried in 1583 an Italian parishioner, Hieronimus Benalius,† known to be a Papist, whose elaborate monument stands in the north aisle, and who ordained a mass to be said for his soul at his native town of Bergamo. It is to Elizabeth's reign also that may be ascribed the late brass to Roger James, brewer, who was buried in the chancel in 1591.

14.—*Parish Government*

During the changes in ecclesiastical doctrine and authority there were simultaneous developments in the form and extent of the parish government in regard to secular affairs. The " masters " of the parish who had bargained with the organ maker for his services in 1519 crystallised into a select vestry of thirty members, whose earliest minutes in 1629 claim that they had existed from time immemorial and who chose the churchwardens, appointed all other parish officers, assessed the church, and poor, rates and administered the church charities.

The earliest poor-rate‡ which exists for the parish dates from 1560 and shows the parishioners paying small sums ranging from 2d. to 12d.

* *Church Deeds*, Nos. 25, 26, 2.
† *P.C.C.*, 36 Butts.
‡ *Church Deeds*, 64

monthly, the vicar, however, paying 20d. quarterly, and eighteen persons receiving poor relief, while 51s. 10d. was paid that year to Christ's Hospital towards the relief of the poor harboured there. Thirteen vestrymen signed the assessment " coleckt in Vestery May the 23, 1562," some of them using their merchant-marks, thus Mr. Smyth expressed his agreement with a fine sketch of a tub.* The poor parishioners who received relief were known as pensioners, and the church papers include petitions addressed to the Masters, Churchwardens and parishioners by the aged who for many years had paid taxes, assesses and all church duties there and had fallen upon evil days.†

Much was expected of the parish even to the finding of suitable houses for the poor. So Faith Bland, a poor widow " destitut of a dwelling-house " begged the churchwardens and assistants for the lease of one of the parish houses promising any rent that " in your grave wisdomes shall seeme meet in Consciens."‡ The condition of poor households in the parish was as scandalous in All Hallows parish as elsewhere in Elizabethan London. In 1579, whilst the curate and churchwardens were seeing to it that the parish had no unorthodox conventicles nor vagrant priests, the constable was making inquiry into sanitary conditions and, after stating with some pride that every house had a chimney, he had to admit that for 57 households, containing in all 85 people, in Tower Street, St. Katherine's Rents and the neighbouring alleys, there were in all only three privies.§ This same report concerned itself also with " inmates " or lodgers, a constant source of trouble to the authorities under the Elizabethan poor law. To protect themselves from future responsibility the churchwardens would take securities from two men of property before allowing a stranger's child to be baptised in the church. So in 1602, two citizens, one a clothworker, the other a fruiterer, gave their bond in £40 to the churchwardens, that the parishioners should have no " costes charges troubles or expences whatsoever " by reason of the " mayden childe of Katheryne the wife of Tirlowe Bryan now resident . . . in the house of Richard Harmon . . . in Beare Yeard," which child the father Thurlow Bryan had recently made suit to the churchwardens to have baptised in the church‖. The expectant mother who was homeless was an even greater trouble to the parish, and the vestry did not scruple to pay her 6d. or 12d. to move on a little farther into the adjacent parish of St. Dunstan's. St. Dunstan's was also called upon in 1643 to contribute towards the relief of many poor in All Hallows parish. The orphans and poor foundlings were given a name by the upper churchwarden, who would often choose to call them " Towers," " Thomas Barkin," " Charles Parish " or " Mark Lane," and sometimes appointed " any beggar " and the grave-digger to stand as godparents in return for a pot of ale. The child was then brought up at the parish expense and as early as possible apprenticed to some master,

* *Church Deeds*, 65.
† *Ibid.*, 5, 79.
‡ *Ibid.*, 27.
§ *Ibid.*, 77.
‖ *Ibid.*, 73.

who would agree to keep him in meat, drink, lodging, apparel and other necessaries, according to the custom of the City of London, and even in exceptional cases to make him free of the city company to which the master himself belonged.*

It was doubtless owing to these duties of the parish authorities that the church has come to possess several private inventories. For instance, it has the account of the household stuff of William Tyldesley which was valued in 1602, and included things of worth such as a " standing bedsted with greie vallance and Curtens," painted cloths in the chamber, and much child-linen, but also numbered several articles lent out to pawn, viz., a half kirtle and a " weding smock " with other things worth 12s., and a petticoat which had been redeemed from goodwife Hewett for 10s. The later church records also include a later redeemed pawn ticket for three shifts, a shirt and a sheet.†

The sudden and extensive fatalities from the plague, which were particularly numerous in the parish in 1563, 1593, 1625 and 1665, added to these responsibilities ; but there is no obvious reason why the parish chest of All Hallows should include the inventory of the goods of William Giles, vicar of Aylesford in Kent, who with his wife and six children died of the " sickness " in 1593. The account shows his extreme poverty. His goods (excluding any beds, which presumably were alone considered to be infected) were worth £13 odd; his debts were assessed at £23 odd. His administrators had paid a poor woman to tend him, his wife and children 12d. a week for 21 weeks, and three others (two of whom seem to have died) for five weeks' attendance on the orphaned children till they died.‡

There is evidence that the Easter offering in 1559 was devoted in part to the poor, for the churchwarden then accounted for 16s. 10d. " received for the paschall towardes the relief of the poore " ;§ but a regular collection was not made to supplement the poor rate until the Commonwealth period, ‖ from which time it appears that the churchwardens and sidesmen stood at the doors and cried " pray remember the poor." The old custom of paying poor men to bear torches or say prayers at funerals survived also in the distribution of money at funerals or marriages which was common in the 17th century.

15.—*Laudian All Hallows* ¶

During the first half of the 17th century there was a definite movement towards beautifying and restoring the church. In 1613, Mr. John Burnell replaced the communion table, which had been bought cheap

* *Ibid.*, 10, 20, 74 ; Maskell, *op. cit.*, p. 121.
† *Ibid.*, 85.
‡ *Ibid.*, 61.
§ *Ibid.*, 25.
‖ *Vestry Min.*, 1647 ; cited by Maskell, *op. cit.*, p. 115.
¶ Based mainly upon the Churchwardens' Accounts.

E

in 1559, with an oak table, doubtless given in memory of his young wife who had died in childbed in 1612. At the same time the parish set up pews and the present pulpit of oak; but the sounding board was too small, and was replaced by the present " pulpitt hedd " made by Mr. Laine in 1638.

In 1616 died the learned vicar, Dr. Robert Tighe, and Archbishop Abbott presented to the living a kinsman of his own, Edward Abbott, whose last years were spent in zealous exhortations and earnest work for the " re-edifying, repaving and beautifying " of the church. In 1626, a silver flagon, weighing 42 oz. 12 dwt. (still in use), was given by Margery Covell, the widow of Francis Covell, citizen and skinner, whose monument remains on the south side of the church. In 1631, Thomas Crathorne gave a silver-gilt cup and cover, and in 1633 Mr. Grimwade added a silver basin. In 1633 the parishioners sold the old plate and pewter, including a silver trencher weighing 6 oz., and the old silver-gilt chalice weighing 19 oz. They thus raised a little more than £7. Then they purchased from Walter Shute, the silversmith, (the present) silver-gilt chalice inscribed " All Hallowes Barking " and weighing 24 oz. 5 dwt. with a cover weighing between eight and nine ounces, and also a silver plate for the communion bread, the present square paten on 4 round knobs, which is said to be unique; they bought also three new pewter flagons, and a new plate " to set the silver flagons on." These included the new flagon given by Edmund Forster that same year.

At the same time, in accordance with a resolution in 1633, a restoration of the building itself began in April 1634. Money was raised by voluntary subscriptions and by gifts from the city companies, the farmers of the Customs and others. About £1400 was expended on these repairs, Mr. Goodwin " the mathematician " being called in as architect.

On Christmas Day, 1634, at the reopening of the church, Edward Abbott preached his " last sweet and swan-like sermon," before his death in March 1635. Thereupon, Archbishop Laud presented to the vicarage a nephew of his own, Edward Layfield, who succeeded in paying off the whole debt for the recent reconstruction of the church. Layfield's compliance with Laud's instructions brought him into conflict with the more Puritanical among his parishioners. In 1638, the Vestry agreed that the " communion Table shd. be sett up to the upper end of the chancell, and that the table shd. be raised one stepp according to order," and paid £52 towards the charges. A hood of black taffety and ten ells of holland for the vicar's surplice were also supplied this year. Next year the Vestry accepted a gift towards a new font from a private donor, and authorised the sale of the old armour (twelve old corselets and head-pieces) to supplement its purchase. This is the existing marble font, the cover of which was a later gift. The Puritans among the parishioners complained to the Bishop of London and to Parliament of these innovations, stating that Dr. Layfield had set the table altar-wise against the east wall of the church, had adorned the chancel with ten statues of saints to which he bowed on going to the altar, had placed a cross over the font and set up the letters I.H.S. in forty places within the church and had refused the sacrament to those who had tried to remove these things by force; for it appears from a later petition that the " little wooden angels " (apparently identical with some of the ten " saints " recited above) were sawn down from the corner of the rail before the communion table.

In December 1640 Laud was impeached of treason and imprisoned in the Tower ; it was the turn of the Puritans to have the support of authority. They petitioned in 1642 for a lecturer to be " allowed the pulpit " on Sunday afternoons and Thursday evenings. The House of Commons ordered Dr. Layfield and his curate to permit certain learned orthodox divines (not necessarily in orders) to preach before the parishioners, so that they might choose a lecturer. On 1st December, 1642, the Puritan parishioners announced to the Commons their choice of Mr. George Cockayne. It follows almost without saying that Dr. Layfield was almost immediately (3rd Feb., 1643) deprived as a delinquent and pronounced incapable of any preferment in the church ; his place was taken by Thomas Clendon, who was appointed by Parliament and signed the audit as vicar in 1643. Dr. Layfield refused to obey the order of deprivation without trial. He was dragged from the church while celebrating divine service, and forced to ride to prison in his surplice with the Book of Common Prayer tied round his neck. Up to the last he was trying to obtain preferment, claiming a canonry in St. Paul's in 1642 ; and he appears to have endeavoured to preserve the cathedral plate, for in 1654 he was said to have certain plate and goods of St. Paul's concealed in his house. It is said that at one time or another he was imprisoned in most of the jails about London, in Ely House and in the galleys on the Thames.*

16.—*Puritan All Hallows*

The parish, like the rest of the country, was divided into factions, but for the time being the Puritan Parliamentarians were in power. In January 1645, three of their enemies who were beheaded on Tower Hill were buried in All Hallows. The register for 1st and 2nd January records the burial of John Hotham, Esq., and Sir John Hotham, Knt., " beheaded for betraying [their] trust to the State," since both had held command in the Parliamentarian forces at Hull, and had plotted their betrayal. On 11th January, Archbishop Laud himself was " decently interred " in a vault beneath the Communion Table of All Hallows with the rites of the Church of England, although these had been abandoned in most of the London churches. He had been beheaded on Tower Hill on the previous day, but the Commons had given permission for the body to be delivered to his servants. One of these was his faithful steward George Snayth, who was buried in the north aisle in 1651. In 1663 Laud's remains were removed to St. John's College, Oxford, in conformity with his wishes. Meantime there had been buried in the chancel near him, the lawyer and soldier, Colonel Eusebius Andrews, who was

* *Cal. S. P. Dom.*, 1641–3, p. 297 ; *Cal. Com. for Advance of Money*, 112 ; Walker, *Sufferings of the Clergy* (ed. Whittaker), 1863, p. 48.

executed as a Royalist on Tower Hill, 22nd August, 1650. His declaration of faith upon the scaffold shows that he was a close follower of Laud.*

The reign of utilitarianism was then in full swing. A " decent basin " for baptisms was bought for All Hallows church in 1645; but Dr. Layfield's " large font of marble stone " was soon restored to the church, for it stood in the middle aisle in 1659. The church became a centre of civil life; Benjamin Shepherd, appointed registrar in 1653, recorded (somewhat unsatisfactorily) births and deaths and the civil marriages performed before Justices of the Peace. The churchyard corner in Tower Street was chosen as a site for the new stocks and whipping-post in 1657. The pews behind the north door were removed in 1645 to make an engine house for Tower Ward. This part of the church long remained a fire-station for the neighbourhood. In the " engine room " in 1659 there stood " one engine marked A^BH with a brass pipe and materials belonging "; while along the north aisle were ranged twenty-four buckets marked " A.B. 1659."

The inventories of the church goods during the Commonwealth show us something of the interior of the church at that time. The communion table had again been moved table-wise and three " forms with backs " were set in the chancel, while another stood under a " turning desk," to which were chained the church books, Fox's *Book of Martyrs*, the works of Dr. Joseph Hall and those of William Perkins, afterwards relegated to the Vestry. One great Bible was left; but the three books of the service according to the Church of England had been " taken by Alderman Andrews." The communion table in 1647 had a new " carpet," or cover, of purple stuff, but the greatest efforts had been made to adorn the pulpit, which besides its red velvet cushion had a " new pulpit cloth and cover . . . with a cushion edged and fringed " of the gift of Mr. Robert Neale. There were nine other green cushions fringed. Prominent in the chancel stood the framed Covenant against Papacy and Prelacy. Yet, strangely enough, the " King's and Prince's " arms remained in the chancel in 1659, and in 1654 the Vestry had set up in one of the windows the arms of England, Scotland, Ireland and London. The church was lighted by sixteen candlesticks, " to set on the pews," and the pulpit by candles in " four joints of brass," possibly each holding four candles, as the inventory of 1634 includes the " great branch of brass containing 16 lights given by Mr. Fras. Covell deceased." Candlesticks were supplemented by lanterns, some of glass, some of horn. Congregations seem to have increased rather than diminished, even though the parishioners were divided as to matters of church discipline and doctrine, for a south gallery was added in 1657.

---

* The religion I profess is that which passeth under the name of Protestant, though that be rather a name of distinction, than properly essential to the religion : but that Religion found out in the Reformation, purged from all the errors of Rome in the reign of Edw. 6, practised in the reign of Elizabeth, James and Charles. . . . that religion, before it was defaced, I am of, which I take to be Christ's catholic, though not the Roman catholic religion. (Cobbett, *State Trials*, V, 42.)

THE PARISH OF ALL HALLOWS BARKING

17.—*The Explosion and Fire of January*, 1649–50

The great parochial event of the Commonwealth was a disaster which befell both church and parish in 1649–50. Numerous accounts relating to this event remain among the church records and many details are included in the Churchwardens' Accounts and Vestry Minutes. At eight o'clock on the evening of Friday, 4th January, happened " a lamentable and fearful fire in a ship-chandler's house by gunpowder." The shopkeeper, Robert Porter, had seven barrels stored in his house in Tower Street for the night, and (fortunately for the parish) had removed twenty more on board ship. The house and four other " fair houses," including the Rose Tavern in Tower Street, were destroyed by the explosion. Ten houses " backward from the street " in Priests Alley were " quite blowne up." Twenty-six others were rendered uninhabitable by the explosion or by the fire which followed and continued until the Saturday morning. The " Vickeridge House " was much shattered. Much damage was done in Chitterling Alley and Beer Lane. The windows of the church " was wholly all broken and blowne out." The church tower was dangerously shaken; but this was not discovered until later.

This " wofull accydent of Powder and Fyer " killed sixty-seven persons or more; many others were badly burned, or left destitute. The landlady and the customers at the Rose were killed or injured, as they were " discoursing on business " at the inn. The landlord was absent and survived. The ship-chandler's family was wiped out. In Priests Alley twenty-four persons were missing.

The care of the destitute and the rebuilding or repair of church and houses were far beyond the means of the parish. The Keepers of the Liberty of England (being the Government of the day) by their Letters Patent allowed collections to be made in all London churches, and the money to be paid in the Vestry House on Tuesday or Thursday in the following week to nine trustees of whom one, William Deacon, a citizen and barber-surgeon, seems to have been particularly active. Two merchants, a gunsmith, a chandler and two " gentlemen " were also upon this committee which received and dispensed the funds for relieving sufferers " by that great blow." Their care in keeping the papers relating to this task, has preserved for us the briefs from more than a hundred city churches, which contributed sums varying from the nine shillings subscribed by the church of St. Andrew by the Wardrobe, to a generous gift of £20 8s. 6d. sent from St. Clement's, East Cheap. By this means £674 odd was collected. The " Honourable Parliament " voted another £200. Six of the city companies gave £41 odd.

These moneys were assigned to the relief of poor sufferers, each one receiving so much from the " Turkey Company Guift," so much from the " Skinners' guift," so much from the " Parliament guift," so much from the " Letters Pattent money," and so on. The sad tales of many of these pensioners have been preserved. Samuel Porter, a scrivener, had lately settled

45

in a house next the Rose Tavern, and had just spent £50 or £60 upon it when it was blown up and the best of all his goods were lost. He was " constrained to betake himself to some Imployment at Sea in ye affaires of the Navy," and his wife, who earned her living by her needle, was " left with her three children to the wide world." Widow Pitts, who had nothing but what she earned by her daily labour, lost goods to the value of £3 4s. Jane Stephens, who lost her husband and child, was greatly concerned because by the former's death she lost all hope of much good which they had expected from a suit at law. Widow Wibourne was aged 100 years, and had lived in the parish for fifty, when the small goods she had left were impaired and spoiled by the disaster. William Knight, a plaisterer, who had lived many years in Chitterling Alley, had his house " utterly ruinated " by " that fatall blowe of gunpowder." Eleanor and Jacob Jezard received £12 10s. towards the loss of £231 odd, which they estimated as the value of their coals and beer, a " Blake Chamlet gowne last with a bone Last," a " blake Tammell gowne Last with 3 Lasses in a seme," a cloth suit with silver buttons, " a Blewe petticote and Schie Coller wascote," plate, pewter, 18 pairs of sheets, pewter brass candlesticks, " Leage horbe boles and other Constante novell waire," three fair looking-glasses and much else. These were of the wealthier sort who suffered. George Robert kept a shop and lost small things blown out of it, and canes " which cost him out of his owne purse at the first peney " £8, besides five gross of ink-horns and two dozen hour-glasses. Henry Thurgood, another shopkeeper, lost two dozen of " knottes and Roses," a dozen of " whited brown thredd " and a dozen of " black and brown." A poor chandler, Richard Prise, not only lost his butter, cheese, soap and candles, but was the worse by divers folk among his debtors who were burnt to death. Presumably Goody (Mary) Fillett, who lived in Priests Alley, also kept a shop, for it is not conceivable that the 24 shirts and smocks, the 11 green and white aprons, the 4 gowns, 14 petticoats and 8 waistcoats, which were destroyed in her house, were all for her own wearing, though the three Bibles and other books for which she sent in a claim may have been a fair allowance for one family. Agnes Hebson, who kept a kind of maternity home, keeping women in childbed for her maintenance, lost her livelihood by the destruction of her house in Beer Lane. Finally, Walter Wormewell, the landlord of the Rose Tavern, " their sad and discontented neighbour," petitioned the trustees to pay for the cure of his man ; but some distrust must have been aroused by the chirurgeon's willingness to reduce his bill from £20 to £6, and Wormewell's discontent was not decreased by any allowance.

The parishioners themselves subscribed £110 for the " reperation of the Church much defaced by the blowe of Gunpowder." Throughout the spring bricklayers, carpenters, plaisterers, plumbers and labourers were at work, clearing the streets and the churchyard of rubbish, putting in 702 feet of glass on the north side of the church, mending the church door, altering pews and setting up rails on the north side of the church, making new leather buckets and repairing the old ones as a precaution against future fires, setting up the churchyard wall, and rebuilding the Vicarage. The

46

opportunity was taken to cleanse the King's arms and the Prince's arms, the Lord's Prayer, Commandments and Belief. A new wall was built at the west end on the south side of the church. The parish tenements, mostly in Priests Alley, were repaired, and much was expended on quarrels of glass and on lead for the casements of the Audit House and other lesser buildings in the parish. For many years the surviving parishioners kept the fourth of January as a day of thanksgiving for their deliverance, collected " thanksgiving " money for the poor, and came together to hear a special sermon.

One bitter memory of the disaster lasted for several years in the acrimonious charges brought by the midwife Hester Shaw against the minister. Among the throngs who on the day following the explosion crowded Thomas Clendon's house in Tower Street, clamouring for their goods which had been brought in thither for safety, were messengers from Mistress Shaw, who came away discontented, feeling that Master Clendon had treated them with anger where they had sought sympathy. The distracted minister hesitated in handing over Mistress Shaw's bags of money, and apparently felt uncertain about the ownership of a certain " silver salt " which proved to be hers. Mistress Shaw frequented many prayer-meetings " in the way of her calling," and in spite of counsel from worthy and notable Puritan divines such as Master Calamy and Master Blackwell, she persisted in repeating her tale that the minister had kept back two bags of money and certain gold rolled in a quilt, and that his daughter had taken one of her new green aprons. Master Clendon attempted to clear himself by an oath taken before the Lord Mayor in 1653, and by publishing an *apologia* prefixed to a sermon upon " Justification Justified." This sermon had been preached in St. Gregory's church in 1652, and was itself too moderate to please the stricter and more " orthodox " divines. Mistress Shaw answered with " Innocency Restored," publishing sworn depositions in her support. Thus the parties tried out in the press a slander case, which under ordinary circumstances would have been heard in the ecclesiastical courts.*

In 1658, it became apparent that the church tower had been so greatly damaged by the explosion that it must either be rebuilt or repaired " for great danger [was] otherwise likely to ensue." In April of that year the Vestry decided to rebuild, accepting the plans of Samuel Twin, bricklayer. Five surveyors examined the old steeple that year; but work did not begin until March 1659, when the bells were taken down. George Lee, probably one of the workmen, was killed by a fall from the steeple, which was then being taken down by Mr. Brathwell. During this year the present brick tower was erected at the end of the nave, the " ould Saintes Bell " was replaced by a new one in the turret, the old peal of five bells was increased to six, and the old clock was replaced by a new one, flanked within the church by two figures of fretwork on each side the dial. Over £200 in voluntary

* Thomas Clendon, *Justification justified . . . in a sermon . . . .* 11 Dec., 1652. London, 1653; Hester Shaw, *Mrs. Shaw's Innocency restored and Mr. Clendon's calumny retorted. . . .* London, 1653; and *A plaine relation of my sufferings by that miserable combustion. . . .* London, 1653.

THE PARISH OF ALL HALLOWS BARKING

gifts were collected towards this work; but its cost was considerably more, and the debt was only paid off after Dr. Layfield's return to the vicarage.

18.—*The Later Growth of the Church and Parish*

Dr. Layfield returned to his old parish shortly after the King came into his own again. His friends among the parishioners greeted him with a festive dinner on 20th October, 1662, and Thomas Clendon, who had supplanted him, retired to the small Essex living of Radminster, where he died.

In 1662 the vicar was once more provided with surplice and hood. But there remained a strong Puritan element among the Vestrymen, and his express wish that the communion table should be replaced altarwise at the east end of the church was only complied with in December 1662, upon an injunction from the Bishop. These were signs of the time. In 1663, the strict Puritans among the Vestrymen were faced with the need for resigning office unless they signed the Declaration of the Act of Uniformity, entailing not only acceptance of the revised Book of Common Prayer, but also renunciation of that Solemn League and Covenant which they had set in so proud a place in the chancel. Fifteen out of the thirty vestrymen declined to sign and may possibly have formed a nucleus for that conventicle of over forty persons, which met in David Austin's house in Tower Hamlet in 1686.* The resignation of just half the vestrymen as a result of the Fourth Act of Uniformity bears out the general impression, obtained from the details of the previous years, that the parishioners were about equally divided between zealous conformity and extreme Puritanism. The remaining fifteen vestrymen proceeded to choose others to bring their number up to thirty. They were faced with a great debt for the recent rebuilding of the church tower, and by difficulties in gathering the money in a divided parish. On Sunday, 23rd April, 1665, after evening prayers the greatest part of the substantial housekeepers with the Doctor [Layfield], churchwardens, and vestrymen appointed twelve persons to assess a rate towards discharging the debt. The churchwarden who ventured to demand the rate on Sir Richard Ford's house in Seething Lane spent an unhappy night in prison, although counsel's opinion was obtained that in the event of refusal the parish might distrain or take action in Court Christian or in the Lord Mayor's court.† Ford, however, who had been knighted for taking part in the city's address to Charles II at the Hague in 1660, was probably too powerful an opponent for this poor churchwarden.

The Great Fire, which began near London Bridge on the night of Saturday, 1st September, 1666, came roaring along Tower Street on the following Tuesday, "coming on in that narrow streete, on both sides, with infinite fury." By the end of the day it had destroyed the Dolphin Tavern,

* *Conventicle Papers* (Guildhall).
† *Church Deed,* 15.

48

THE PARISH OF ALL HALLOWS BARKING

part of the church property ;* but about here the blowing up of houses with gunpowder, and the help given by workmen from the King's Yards checked its progress. It was thus due to Sir William Penn, the distinguished admiral then in residence at the Navy Office, that All Hallows was saved from the fire, " it having burned the dyall of Barking Church, and part of the porch, and was there quenched." This was by the Wednesday, when Samuel Pepys went " up to the top of Barking steeple " . . . and thence watched the " great fires, oyle-cellars and brimstone and other things burning " until he " became afeared to stay there long and down again as fast as I could."† The church, indeed, had a very narrow escape, and the vicarage which stood against its south-west corner in Tower Street was destroyed, and was subsequently rebuilt by Dr. Layfield.

Pepys and Penn were not themselves parishioners of All Hallows, as they both lived at the Navy Office at the top of Seething Lane in St. Olave's parish. William Penn, the admiral's son and founder of Pennsylvania, had, however, been baptized at All Hallows in 1644. Pepys attended All Hallows only on special occasions. For instance, on 9th October, 1664, when the " wit of Cambridge," Mr. Fuller, preached " well and neatly " a sermon which must have had brevity as well as wit, for the Diarist was out in time for service at St. Olave's, and so was able to follow home from there " one of the prettiest women he ever saw." Pepys did not even attend the funeral of his " Morena," the " pretty black girl " Elizabeth Dekins, but listened in bed to the bells of All Hallows tolling for her burial on the night of 22nd October, 1662.‡ In 1667, Sarah Neesham was here married in a fit of generous gratitude by George Jeffreys, then a young lawyer, and destined to gain notoriety as a brutal judge and Lord Chancellor.

Towards the end of Charles II's reign, steps were taken to make the church and its services more beautiful. In 1675, Renatus Harris was employed to install an organ in the West Gallery, the old organ having probably disappeared during the Commonwealth. In the alterations which ensued the clock dial with its fretwork figures of Time and Death were moved into the church, and the figure which had stood between Time and Death was moved by the churchwarden (Mr. Clements) to the east end, where it was set up over the commandments. This was " a Great, Carved, Guilded Image, and about a yard and a half long, with great, broad, spreading wings, . . . the right Arm and Hand holding a Trumpet near to its mouth, the left . . . holding . . . a Label of Lead . . . on the Label *Arise you dead, and come to judgment.*" Shortly afterwards one of the parishioners gave the church a rich " carpet " or frontal embroidered with a *Glory* and the letters I.H.S. About the same time, the lecturer, Mr. Jonathan Saunders, began to introduce more ceremony into his conduct of the services. These things gave offence to many coming as they did at a time when the popular mind,

* *Ibid.*, 68.
† *Diary* (ed. Wheatley) V, 425, 426.
‡ *Ibid.*, iv, 262 ; ii, 372.

stirred to anti-Romanism by the intrigues of Titus Oates, converted all forms and ceremonies into Papistry. Presentments were made at the Old Bailey against this image " of St. Michael," and in 1681, the senior churchwarden, Edmund Sherman, having been indicted with others for allowing it to remain in the church, gave serious offence by his arbitrary actions, firstly by carrying off the image to the trial, secondly by pleading guilty contrary to the vicar's advice, and thirdly by making firewood of the figure for the vestry meetings. Meantime, the vicar, Dr. Hickes, had bound himself to traverse an indictment in the same matter at the sessions following; and the indictment was then quashed on the ground that offences violating the Edwardian Statute against images could not be tried save by Justices of Assize or of the Peace. The lecturer took up cudgels on behalf of the burned image, publishing two pamphlets on the "Apparitions" at Barking. Sherman's disrespect for the lecturer seems to have been compounded of a real disapproval of his novel ceremoniousness, and of jovial contempt for a neighbour with whom he had been " very merry at Tavern dinner last Election-day *secundum usum Barkin.*" He answered the " Apparitions " in two clever but scurrilous pamphlets on " The Birth and Burning of St. Michael," and so the matter came to rest.*

The parishioners as a whole were evidently disinclined to support Sherman, and in 1686, the figure having been destroyed, Mr. John Richardson gave the present altar-piece, of classical design, with its pictures of Moses and Aaron and with the tables of the Commandments and the Lord's Prayer usual in the city churches rebuilt after the Great Fire. At the same time a new communion table was given by Major Richard Burdon. In the midst of the dispute, in 1682, Mr. James Foyle gave the present font-cover which has been ascribed to Grinling Gibbons, while Mr. George Crosley supplied the iron branch to support it. The cover cost £12; the branch £3.

The learned vicar who bore a dignified part in these contentions was Dr. George Hickes, who had recently been appointed to All Hallows, and resigned the living in 1686, being then Dean of Worcester. He afterwards lost all his preferments in 1689 upon refusing the oath of allegiance to William and Mary and turned physician to earn his daily bread; some years later he was one of the two Jacobean bishops consecrated at Enfield in order to continue the episcopal succession among non-jurors. Even before his appointment to All Hallows he had been connected with the neighbourhood, for in 1668 he had come courting a Mrs. Howell at the Navy Office and had preached at St. Olave's, Hart Street, a sermon which Samuel Pepys found " but dull."†

In 1695, All Hallows gave a resting-place to another famous non-juror, the devout and learned John Kettlewell, who had been an intimate friend of George Hickes and was buried in the tomb that had been Arch-

---

* Edmund Sherman, *The Birth and Burning of the Image called St. Michael.* London, 1681.
† *Diary,* ed. Wheatley, viii, 108, 214.

THE PARISH OF ALL HALLOWS BARKING

bishop Laud's. The burial service was read by Bishop Ken himself, who (though a non-juror) officiated upon this occasion in episcopal vestments and prayed for the King and queens [*sic*].*

During the last century or so parish life has undergone far-reaching changes. One of the greatest was the dwindling of the Vestry's power. At All Hallows the old "select" Vestry, whose records date back to 1629, readily accepted the new order of things, and at a meeting in the church in 1808 opened the election of its members to parishioners at large. It is to the Vestry's credit that this was done without the litigation which brought about the same changes elsewhere. The diversity of the church's duties in former days is reflected in its records. These include, for instance, the Workhouse Accounts, with a wealth of detailed expenditure upon Godfrey's cordial, Penny Royal, Juniper Berries and " Miselto," and also the rates for maintaining firecocks and the fire-engine, which was housed at the church. Later, in common with all parishes, the Vestry lost its civil duties, particularly the administration of poor relief, so that to-day its chief function is the choice of churchwardens.

The medieval " masters " of the parish managed secular and ecclesiastical business together, and never dreamed of severing them, for in their guilds and in their daily lives religion and trade were inextricably mingled. The modern Parochial Council, chosen by all enrolled communicants, has a more democratic constitution; but its business is more strictly limited to church matters. This is one result of the general tendency to separate religious from secular business, and this general tendency to segregate spiritual life has been intensified in city parishes, such as All Hallows, by the gradual replacement of crowded dwelling-houses by the office and the warehouse. In 1801 the parishioners numbered 2087; now there are barely 200.

More than once of late times, the large endowment of this important but sparsely-populated parish has been used for work of wider scope than that of a parish church. In 1884, All Hallows became the mission church of a small college of priests which was established in Trinity Square. In 1922, it became the Guild Church of Toc H, whose common ideals of service and comradeship are based upon memories of the Great War, and especially upon the social work then done by Talbot House in Poperinghe. The association of the church with this movement was confirmed in 1928 by the creation of an All Hallows Toc H Trust under a joint deed of the Archbishop of Canterbury, as patron, and the Corporation of Toc H. The Anglican padres were thereby given a special collegiate connexion, and a Collegiate House has been re-established (1929), at 42 Trinity Square. The increase in communicants from 1092 in 1922 to the present-day number of 7382 indicates the modern growth in the spiritual work of the church, which by means of Toc H is further extended throughout the Empire and beyond.

* H. P. K. Skipton, *The Non-jurors* (1917), p. 33.

II.—THE RECTORS AND AFTERWARDS VICARS OF ALL HALLOWS BARKING

The list is that of Hennessey's *Novum Repertorium Ecclesiasticum* brought up to date.

Rectors.

JOHN DE S. MAGNUS	1269	
WILLIAM DE GATTEWICKE	1292	
GILBERT DE WYGETON		1312
WALTER GRAPYNELL	1317/8	1331
MAURICE DE JENNINGE	1333	
JOHN FOUCHER		1351/2
NICHOLAS JANING	1351/2	
THOMAS DE BROKE	1363	1366
THOMAS DE DALBY	1376	1379/80
LAURENCE DE KAGRER	1379/80	

Vicars.

WILLIAM COLLES	1387/8	1389/90
ROBERT COTON	1389/90	1390
NICHOLAS BROMESGROVE	1390	1416
JOHN HARLYSTON	1419	
JOHN CLERKE		1427
WILLIAM NORTHWOLD	1427	1431/2
JOHN IFORD	1431/2	1434/5
THOMAS VYRBY	1434/5	1454
JOHN MACHEN	1454	1458
JOHN WYNE	1458	
THOMAS CAAS	1468	1475/6
ROBERT SEGRYM	1475/6	1478
RICHARD BALDRY, A.M.	1478	1485
WILLIAM TALBOT, D.D.	1485	
EDMUND CHATTERTON	1492	1493
RALPH DERLOVE	1493	1504
WILLIAM GEDDING	1504	1512
WILLIAM PATTENSON	1512/3	1525
ROBERT CARTER, S.T.B.	1525	1530
JOHN NAYLOR	1530	1542
WILLIAM DAWES, LL.B.	1542	1565
RICHARD TYRWHIT	1565	1584/5
RICHARD WOOD, S.T.P.	1584/5	1591
THOMAS RAVIS, S.T.B.	1591	1598

THE PARISH OF ALL HALLOWS BARKING

Vicars—continued

ROBERT TIGHE, S.T.B.	1598	1616
EDWARD ABBOTT, A.M.	1616	1634
EDWARD LAYFIELD, A.M.	1634	1680
GEORGE HICKS, S.T.P.	1680	1686
JOHN GASKARTH, A.M.	1686	1732
WILLIAM GEEKLE	1732/3	1767
GEORGE STINTON	1767	1783
SAMUEL JOHNES, KNT.	1783	1852
JOHN THOMAS, B.C.L.	1852	1883
ARTHUR JAMES MASON	1884	1895
ARTHUR WILLIAM ROBINSON	1895	1917
CHARLES EDMUND LAMBERT	1917	1922
PHILIP THOMAS BYARD CLAYTON	1922	

III.—ARCHITECTURE

(1) *General Description*

The Parish Church of All Hallows Barking stands on the north side of Great Tower Street. The walls are of ragstone and other rubble with dressings of limestone; the tower is of brick; the roofs are covered with slate and lead.

The church has a particular interest because it is one of the few London churches that escaped the Great Fire; but the cumulative effect of a series of drastic restorations has been very largely to obliterate the structural evidences of the development of the building.

Of the church given by Riculf to the monks of Rochester in the 12th century, or of any earlier building, there are no certain traces. Further research may, however, at a future date throw light upon architectural remains which have been recently revealed. The probable extent of Riculf's church covered the present Nave and the first two bays of the Chancel. Whether it had aisles it is impossible to say.

As far as one can judge, this Norman church was entirely rebuilt in the 13th century. The new church certainly had aisles, and the earliest parts of the present structure are the north and south arcades of the Nave which differ slightly in detail, but appear to date from about the middle of the 13th century or perhaps earlier, while the east wall is probably of early 14th-century date, and this is in all likelihood also the period of the framework of the much-restored east window which escaped the rebuilding in 1634–5, referred to later.

The next addition to the 13th-century structure may have been the extension of its north and south aisles as far as the first pier from the east end of the existing Chancel. This position is suggested by the comparative narrowness of the eastern arches of the Chancel.

The existence of the recently discovered Crypt, under the east end of the South Chapel (which is probably work of the middle of the 14th century) shows that the Chancel had at least a South Chapel, and there may have been a similar one on the north side, both of narrower breadth than the present Chapels. At the entrance to the Chancel traces have been discovered of a wall running north and south which perhaps indicates the site of the original Chancel arch.

About the middle of the 15th century the North (?) and South Chapels were rebuilt and widened and the present north and south arcades of the Chancel inserted; at the same time the eastern bays of the Nave arcades had their spans increased by the setting eastwards of their eastern responds which were rebuilt and incorporated with the western responds of the Chancel arcades. The date is substantiated by the will of John Cok, who died in 1440 and bequeathed a sum of money for " new building " provided that the work was started within two years. Money for reconstructing the church roof had been given in 1410.* The north and south aisles of the Nave are also of the 15th century, and they were almost certainly widened and extended westwards when the 13th-century aisles were removed.

Other work of the 15th or early 16th century includes the raising of the Clearstorey and the consequent heightening of the east wall. In 1547† church plate was sold to the value of £77, and £37 was spent in repairing the church.

In 1634–5 the Nave arcades were remodelled, their appearance being altered by the fitting of new capitals to most of the columns and responds which were heightened about two feet. We have already been told how the work was done under Mr. Goodwin, the mathematician. It included the " making newe " of all the upper windows and several side windows, painting and gilding the Nave roof (which seems to have been a new one throughout) and the resetting of the glass in the great east window. All this was done with outside advice. Mr. Stone, the King's Surveyor, gave his help in return for his score at the Rose Tavern, and for a " roundlett of canarie wine " costing £1 8s. In the collection of the London County Council are two pencil sketches (Plate 19) by J. Carter, dated 1770. They show the old ceiling and the new one constructed at that date (see below).

In 1649–50 the church was injured by the terrible explosion near its south side (see p. 45). The tower was much shaken and nine years afterwards had to be taken down, a new tower at the west end of the nave being built in 1658–9. The position of the old steeple is rather uncertain. The map ascribed to Agas shows it at the end of the south aisle, so does Faithorne's view, drawn probably between 1643 and 1647, also Hollar's large view published at Antwerp in the latter year. Maskell on page 24 of his account says: " The site of the steeple was changed from the west end of the south aisle to the west end of the nave." Again, in a recent digging close to the present tower, no remains of medieval foundations came to light. On the other hand, the present clearstorey window at the south-west end of the nave, unless it be a later insertion, hardly leaves room for a south-west steeple, and the bird's-eye view of the Tower of London and its neighbourhood by Haiward and Gascoyne, 1597 (see illustration before text), shows the steeple at the end of the nave.‡

In 1704–5 the south gallery was taken down and the organ gallery enlarged, pews over 4 ft. high being erected. The organ was again enlarged in 1720, when a choir organ was added. A Committee for Repairs was set up in 1769, and between that year and 1778 the roof of the Nave was lowered and slated, painted and gilded. The aisle roofs were slated and new-ceiled. The pews of the churchwardens and overseers were removed and the altar-piece was painted and coloured.

The East Vestry was probably added about the end of the 17th

* See Historical Description, p. 10.
† *Ibid.*, p. 36.
‡ Leake's plan, engraved by Hollar, 1667, shows what is evidently intended to be the new tower, but standing at the west end of the south aisle.

century or later, when the fittings of the church were renewed. The earliest reference found to a Vestry is in the will of Thomas a Wode, who desired in 1468 to be buried in the churchyard of All Hallowe Berkyng of London in the " place where ye westiary is."*

A drastic modern restoration was that of 1814 when no less than £5313 was expended. A new peal of eight bells cost in all £653 12s., and the Nave roof was renewed in deal and plaster, but apparently on somewhat similar lines to the " new ceiling " sketched by Carter in 1770, the Vestry was altered and the walls of the church generally were lowered. The battlements shown by West and Toms (Frontispiece) had disappeared by 1803 (see Whichelo's Drawing, Plate No. 2). Other restorations took place in 1836.

In 1862–3 the widening of Tower Street caused the destruction of the Vicarage which Dr. Layfield had rebuilt at the south-west corner of the church. A south porch and south doorway were then removed, the latter resembling in style the present north doorway. An octagonal Turret leading up to the roof and perhaps to a room over the Porch was also cut off (see Plate No. 16), but inside the church the Turret doorway can still be seen. The south wall of the Churchyard was then set back by 10 feet and the wall on the north and that on the east in Barking Alley by four feet.

In 1883, soon after the Rev. A. J. Mason (now Canon Mason, D.D.) became Vicar, very important alterations were taken in hand under the direction of the late Mr. J. L. Pearson, architect, and continued during many years. A high-pitched roof was placed over the Nave, the aisles were re-roofed, and the organ gallery altered. There was already a modern brick building over the Porch. This was removed, as well as two shops to the west of it, and at Canon Mason's expense the present important stone structure was added, extending on each side of the porch and having one storey above it. To judge from the preface to a pamphlet called *Berkyinge-chirche All Hallows by the Tower* (1927) the work of restoration was in progress from 1884 to 1895.

(2) *Detailed Description*

Chancel   The Chancel (39½ ft. by 24 ft.) has an east window of five lights and a traceried two-centred head in the style of the early 14th century. The internal splayed jambs are in part ancient, but the mullions and tracery are modern restorations possibly on the old lines.

The east wall dates from the same century, and in its south part contains a doorway (below the window) which is probably of late 17th- or early 18th-century date opening into the East Vestry.

In the side walls of the Chancel are mid-15th-century arcades of three bays, the easternmost bay on each side having a two-centred arch, the others being four-centred. While the easternmost arch on the north side is slightly lower than its fellow, that on the opposite wall is slightly higher, the string courses marking the base of the Clearstorey stepping downwards

* *Comm. Lond.*, 36 Wilde.

56

and upwards respectively above these arches. The cause of these breaks in the levels is not now evident.

The arches are symmetrically moulded, having on each face a central filleted roll, flanked by deep casements dividing it from the innermost and outermost orders, which consist of a hollow chamfer and an ogee mould. The responds and piers are composed of round shafts separated by hollows and enclosing a filleted roll which is continuous with those of the arches. The shafts have moulded capitals (changing in the bell from a round to a semi-octagonal plan) and moulded bases, with semi-octagonal sub-bases on plinths. The arches have moulded labels towards the Chancel which mitre at the top with the string course of the Clearstorey.

The Clearstorey is lighted on each side by three windows; the easternmost is of two and the others of three lights, all under four-centred heads with segmental pointed rear arches. Their design is probably contemporary with the Chancel, but they were renewed in the 17th century, with Mr. Goodwin, the mathematician, as architect; £400 was expended upon the work.

The North Chapel (or Chancel aisle), 19½ feet wide, has an east window of four lights under a segmental pointed head; the jambs and mullions are moulded, the former having a comparatively deep casement. In the second and third bays of the north wall are similar windows, but these are of three lights. All have external hood moulds. They were renewed probably in the 17th century and again to some extent later.

The South Chapel (20 feet wide) has an east window and three south windows similar to those of the North Chapel, but differing slightly in the internal mouldings of the jambs.

It is interesting to note that, whereas the windows in the north aisle have obtusely pointed heads, those on the south side are rounded. It is probable that the south aisle may have suffered rather badly in the great explosion of 1649, and that wholesale repair of the damage at that time accounts for the slight deviation in style.

The Nave (57 feet average by 24 feet) is undivided structurally *Nave* from the Chancel. It has north and south arcades, the northern and longer arcade being of four bays, the southern of three, the difference being caused by the encroachment of the south-west building next the church. The arcades date from about 1230–40, and differ slightly in workmanship, that on the south having three chamfers, while there are only two on the north side, though both arcades are really of two orders. They retain their cylindrical columns, but there are indications that some of them may have been rebuilt later. The westernmost column and the west respond of the north arcade and the western respond of the south arcade (which seems to have been rebuilt in the 15th century) retain the original 13th-century bell capitals, but the other columns have had their original capitals removed and have been heightened some 2 feet and fitted with moulded capitals of early 17th-century date. These are raised above the original springing levels at the expense of the arches which lost their springing stones when this

F

work was carried out.* The arches are pointed and of two chamfered orders. It is noticeable that the easternmost bay on either side is of wider span than the others. This was probably caused by the displacement of the 13th-century responds when the 15th-century Chancel arcades were built, but may have had a practical reason in the accommodation of the rood-loft and screen.† The existing responds correspond with the circular columns of the arcade, but the stone courses continue through with those of the Chancel arcades and are rather deeper than the 13th-century coursing. When this alteration was carried out the moving of the responds eastwards necessitated a rebuilding of the arches. On the north side only the eastern half of the arch appears to have been reconstructed, thus throwing the apex out of centre and giving the whole arch a rather distorted appearance. But on the south side perhaps rather more than half the arch was rebuilt, making it almost a four-centred one, instead of two-centred, with the apex more or less central.

All the other arches appear to have been rebuilt either in the 15th or early in the 16th century (certainly before the early 17th-century changes), but a number of the original small voussoirs of the 13th century are incorporated in this work. The bases of the columns have been cut away.

The Clearstorey has on either side a 15th-century moulded string course above the arcade, and is lighted by four windows on each side, uniform with those of the Chancel. They are very much restored.

Aisles The north and south aisles of the Nave are structurally continuous with the North and South Chapels, and their windows correspond in detail with those described above. The north aisle has a window in each of the first two bays, but not set centrally, and a doorway behind the panelling in the first bay, which doubtless gave access to the Rood. In the third bay is a 15th-century doorway which has a four-centred arch under a square head with a moulded label. The spandrels of the head are quatre-foiled and carved, the eastern with a lozenge-shaped flower, the western with a rose. In the fourth bay is a blocked window not visible internally, but with the exterior exposed inside the modern chamber which covers the bay. A window, similar to that in the east, occupies the west wall, which on plan is canted outwards from north to south so as to continue the line of the Tower, thus causing an irregular addition to the fourth bay in line with the north arcade. The wall here is carried on a segmental arch blocked by the north wall of the Tower, and the respond suggests the termination of the 13th-century Nave. The fourth bay and this extension are cut off from the aisle to form a Vestry to the north of the Tower, which has a modern doorway opening into the modern north-west addition. The south aisle has two windows similar to those of the South Chapel in the first two bays. The third or westernmost bay has been mutilated by cutting off the south-west corner when Tower Street was widened in 1862–3. It is built on the cant and contains the modern

---

* See Goodwin's Work in 1634–5. See pp. 42, 55.
† See Historical Notes, p. 37.

58

THE PARISH OF ALL HALLOWS BARKING

south entrance (referred to on page 56). In this bay, east of the entrance, is a smaller doorway of the 15th century of plain detail with a four-centred arch. This has been recently disclosed by the removal of the wall panelling, and at one time opened into the staircase which led to the roof or perhaps to an upper room above the South Porch which was removed about 1862–3.* The west wall has no windows.

The present Tower (9½ ft. by 11 ft.), built in 1659, is of brick and *Tower* is of four stages, marked externally by brick bands, and is finished with a modern plain parapet. The Tower is not placed centrally with the Nave and lines with the canted west wall of the north aisle, its axis thus making a noticeable deviation to the north from that of the Nave; it is also considerably narrower than the Nave.

The ground-stage has, in the east wall, a round-headed archway opening into the Nave, and in the west wall a round-headed doorway above which is a small oval window, both included internally under one square head. Externally the doorway has plain raised imposts and key block, and the window is set in a simple rectangular architrave.

The circular staircase of timber is set in a semicircular sinking in the south-west angle of the Tower walls, the inner semicircle being protected only by an open wood framing. The second stage has in the west wall a round-headed window with a wooden frame and two pointed and transomed lights. The third stage has a similar west window. The bell-chamber has in each face a round-headed louvred opening with wooden frame and two transomed lights. Set on the centre of the Tower is a square timber lantern or cupola covered with lead and having two round-headed lights on each face. The lantern has a moulded cornice and a square dome with a ball and weather-vane at the top.

The Crypt, under the east half of the South Chapel, was opened out *Crypt* in 1927, and is now fitted up as a Chapel. It is probably of mid-14th-century date. It has a semicircular barrel vault, divided into five narrow bays by chamfered ribs of stone, the in-filling being of chalk, which is also the material of the side walls (north and south). In the east wall is an 18th- or 19th-century doorway, the north jamb of which is of brick and the south jamb a rebated one of older stone—possibly the remains of an earlier doorway *in situ*. It opens into a small brick lobby from which a stairway rises to the level of the churchyard outside.

In the south wall, in the second bay from the east, is an original window of roughly chamfered stones with its rear arch groined back to the main vault. In the next bay westward are the sill and lower jamb stones of another single light, but inside the crypt the groined rear-vault has been filled in with chalk, flush with the main vault.

In the west wall, at its north end, is an original doorway, the dressings of which have been removed or have perished, now restored in chalk. From this doorway is an original straight stairway with much-perished steps

* There is a similar turret at St. Andrew Undershaft leading on to the roof.

which led up to the interior of the church, west of the Crypt. It is now closed over with old paving.

At the south end of the west wall is a 17th- or 18th-century opening into a small lobby of brick with a round vault also of brick, and south of the Crypt is a long narrow chamber forming a 17th-century burial vault of brick. This has a deep niche at its east end.

From the west end of the last chamber are modern steps leading up into the south aisle.

Vestry   The Vestry at the east end of the Chancel was built probably late in the 17th or early in the 18th century, but it has been completely altered and the walls rendered in cement. It has three modern windows in the east and a modern doorway in the south wall.

Recent   Excavations, made under the Nave and Tower of the church in 1928,
Excavations revealed certain interesting features. Under the east end of the Nave a number of very fragmentary rubble foundations were encountered, which were too formless to give any sure indication of their former significance. Under the gallery at the west end, was found a square pier of mixed rubble set in the middle of a square enclosure of brick, leaving a space about two feet wide around the pier. The materials of the pier indicated that it was not older than the 17th century and may well have been much later Its position suggests the base for a Font, but the depth of the foundation (15 feet below the present floor-level) and the presence of the surrounding enclosure would seem to negative this explanation. Under the tower and extending into the Nave was found a considerable extent of Roman pavement consisting of plain red tesseræ, apparently all belonging to one apartment but cut across by the foundation of the east wall of the Tower and (so far) with no trace of an edge or enclosing wall of the same date on any side.

(3) *Fittings*

WITH THE EXCEPTION OF MEMORIAL BRASSES AND MONUMENTS WHICH
WILL BE INCLUDED IN THE SECOND VOLUME

Alms box.

In brass—from Christ's Hospital. On a fluted tapering brass pedestal with moulded cap and base. The sides of the box are enriched with roundels and leaves in relief. The top has two slots and an upright division between them with semi-circular top. On the upper portion of both sides of this division a shield, with the arms of Christ's Hospital and beneath it an inscription. On the one side—

> *It is better to give than to receive*

on the other—

> *Let your light so shine before Men that they may see your good Works and Glorify your Father which is in Heaven.*

60

The top of the box is inscribed—

THE GIFT OF A GOVERNOUR
SEP^T 21ST 1787

Chairs.

Two. In Chancel, of oak with richly carved backs having an up-holstered centre panel, enriched frame, and turned posts with carved heads and finials. The legs are turned and have scalloped feet with a shaped and carved stretcher—late 17th century.

Cistern.

On the north side of the Tower, of lead with panelled and enriched sides, bearing a lion's head and two shields with initials A^BH. The date, 1705, is placed above the panels.

Clock.

On the west face of the Tower, a carved and enriched wooden clock-case with scrolls and pediment, having a curved bracket under the supporting beam—late 17th century.

Communion rails.

Of brass with moulded rails, symmetrically turned balusters and rectangular standards, given by Ann Colleton, who died 1741.

Communion table.

Of oak with moulded and carved upper and lower rails, supported at each end by a centre post flanked by carved scrolls above and two carved eagles on pedestals, with additional brackets on the cross rail and stretcher—*circa* 1685. There was an earlier table presented in 1613, at which date the furniture of the church underwent complete renewal.

Doors.

Doors and lobbies to north and south entrances. The panelled north door and those to the inner lobby are now glazed and the latter have fanlights over; the inner doorways are flanked by fluted Corinthian pilasters with an entablature; the sides of the lobbies are panelled—1705.

In the doorway leading to the stairway in the turret, removed about 1862–3, is a door with feathered battens and two plain strap hinges—probably 16th century.

Easter Sepulchre.

The altar tombs in the North and South Chancel Chapels are of a form which was often in use as an Easter Sepulchre, although not necessarily built for that purpose. These will be described under Monuments in the second volume, but it may be mentioned that the one to the south of the Chancel has remains of a brass representing the Resurrection.

61

Font and cover.

The font is a moulded bowl, of dark grey marble, with baluster-shaped stem and square moulded base. In 1645 it is recorded " the then font was moved from the church and replaced by a decent basin." The cover is an exceptionally fine piece of carving. Its baseboard is circular, and there appears to have been at one time an inscription on the rim containing the words " . . . Kingdom of God "; above it the cover is formed of a pyramid of oak, crowned by a dove; around this are grouped freely carved festoons of fruit and flowers, the ends divided and spreading over the baseboard; between the festoons are three finely modelled amorini. The wrought-iron bracket is of scroll and leaf work and supports the cover by means of a pulley and counterweight, the latter being moulded and chased with a floral pattern—*circa* 1705, or perhaps late 17th century.

Gallery.

The gallery at the west end has a modern front; it retains its old staircase with turned balusters, square newel, moulded rail, and uncut moulded string.

Glass.

In the north wall, a panel in the second window. In the south wall, panels in second and easternmost windows, and fragments in fourth and fifth windows.

A full description is given on page 65.

Hat or cloak pegs.

The decorative iron frame with hat or cloak pegs on either side of it, affixed to the pillar of the north arcade at the back of the pulpit, was perhaps in the pew of some rich citizen.

Images.

Two of oak, a gift in 1929. The one of St. James is about 4 feet high and probably medieval. The other is smaller and said to be St. Hubert, but might be St. Roche.

Organ-case.

The original case remains and the pipes are contained in three towers, the centre one being square in plan, and the side ones circular. They are carried on a moulded shelf which follows the shape, and beneath those at the side are moulded corbels supported by cherub heads. The upper part of each tower has an elaborate entablature with enriched frieze and sections of pierced work clasp the ends of the pipes. The spaces between the towers have two tiers of smaller pipes, the lower being so arranged as to permit of fine panels of pierced scrollwork. The upper ones finish with a cornice ramped up to the centre tower and support two seated figures of angels with trumpets. There is a band of carving beneath the overhanging case, and the work below is composed of plain modern panelling which was erected at the reconstruction by Harrison and Harrison of Durham, in 1909. Maskell records it was originally erected by Renatus Harris at a total cost of £306 8s. 10d., of which Harris received £220—date 1675-7.

Painting.

Newly fixed on reredos ; the Holy Trinity, SS. John the Baptist, Zacharias, and Elizabeth. Now concealed by curtain hangings.

Panelling.

There is panelled wainscoting all round the church with moulded capping, also unset panelling of which the partitions at the west end of the north aisle are formed—*circa* 1705. Part of the moulded capping on the north wall under the third window is of stone. (See also Screens, etc.)

Piscina.

In the Chancel (south-east respond). It has a damaged cinque-foiled ogee head, Credence shelf, and part of a round basin—15th century.

Plate.

The Plate (silver) includes a flagon of 1627, representing a gift of 1626, inscribed " *The Gift of Mrs. Margery Couell*, A.D. 1626 "; a flagon of 1633, given in 1634, inscribed " *Edmundus Forster* 1634 "; a cup and cover paten of 1631, given in the same year, inscribed " *Ex dono Thomae Crathorne 24 Decembris* 1631 "; a cup and cover paten, marked 1633 and dated 1634, inscribed " *All Hallows, Barking, Anno Domini* 1634 "; a small cup marked 1684, dated 1685, inscribed " *All Saints Berkin London* 1685 "; a square paten of 1633; a dish of 1633, dated the same year, inscribed " *All Hallows, Barking* 1633," and a spoon, probably of late 16th-century date, of which the end, possibly a seal, has been cut off.

A Beadle's Staff, pear-shaped, of silver, inscribed " *All Hallows, Barking*, 1800."

The Tankards are plain, the square paten unique.

Pulpit.

Of oak, hexagonal, handsomely carved. It possesses a moulded entablature and base, each face consisting of two panels divided into two parts, the lower with a draped swag and the upper with an elaborate tablet inset having a roundheaded panel in the centre beneath a carved and scrolled pediment. At each angle are two carved and enriched terminal pilasters. The whole is supported upon an ogee stem, with moulded ribs springing from the moulded capping of the post—early 17th century. The staircase has a moulded handrail of scrolled and foliated ironwork of great beauty—*circa* 1705.

Above the Pulpit is an equally fine hexagonal sounding-board, placed there twenty-five years after the erection of the pulpit. It has a panelled soffit on which is a wreath of bay leaves. The enriched entablature has cherub head pendants at the angles and a panelled tablet with painted

63

inscription "*Xpm p̄dcam crucifixum* * *" on the middle of each face, the frieze being carved with fruit, etc. It is supported by a panelled back with pierced arabesque scrolls and cherub heads. The pulpit dates from 1613, and the sounding-board was bought in 1638. (See Vestry minutes.)

Recess.

In north wall under the third window, concealed by panelling but with the east jambs still visible—probably 15th century.

Reredos.

Of three main bays, divided and flanked by fluted Corinthian columns, supporting a continuous enriched entablature, which breaks forward above the columns and was once surmounted by four draped urns. The middle bay has, at the base, a panel of carved scrolled foliage; the side bays have each a round-headed panel with paintings of Moses and Aaron respectively, and below each is carved a cherub's head and swags, on a console panel. Flanking the reredos are further enriched panels inscribed with the Lord's Prayer and Creed, framed in carved swags and festoons and finished with segmental pediments; below each is a panelled door, one leading into the Vestry, but the other being a sham—the whole dates from 1686.

Royal Arms.

On east side of gallery facing Nave, Stuart arms of carved wood, perhaps those mentioned on p. 44 as " remaining in the chancel."

Screens.

Now in various positions in the Sanctuary. These panelled screens have a fine series of carved and pierced frieze panels, beneath a carved and moulded capping; at one end there are panelled projections formed like buttresses, each finished with pierced and carved scrolls. These screens date from about 1705 and originally stood across the Nave from which they separated the eastern half bay.

Around the font a part panelled enclosure with gates and front rails having turned balusters—*circa* 1705.

Seating.

The pews generally are early 18th century and panelled, but cut down and altered. The churchwardens' enclosed pews at the west end of the Nave have pierced and carved frieze panels in front, and a fine series of solid carved panels at the back, four of which contain medallions with figures in low relief of the Evangelists. In the south pew are two seats with carved arm-rests. Elsewhere in the church are a number of settles and forms, 32 in all, of varying lengths, some with and the others without backs. Two are curved in plan and they all are of late 17th or early 18th century.

* " *Christum praedicam crucifixum.*"

THE PARISH OF ALL HALLOWS BARKING

Sword-rests.

Three, now on a screen containing old carved panels on the north side of the Chancel, behind the choir seats, of scrolled and foliated ironwork. Erected respectively in honour of Sir John Eyles, Bart., Lord Mayor, 1727, with arms of the Haberdashers' Company; of Slingsby Bethell, M.P. for London and Lord Mayor in 1755, with arms of the Salters' Company; and of Sir Thomas Chitty, Lord Mayor, 1760, with arms of the Fishmongers' Company. It is recorded in the Vestry minutes 23 October, 1755, that " it be left to the churchwardens to alter the Corporation Pew in the church for the reception of Slingsby Bethell, Esq., Lord Mayor elect, in the same manner as it was done in the Mayoralty of Sir John Eyles and to provide a handsome sword-iron with proper arms and decorations."

Eyles

Miscellanea.

In bell-chamber, enriched wooden panel recording the erection of the Tower in 1659.

Bethell

(4) *Ancient Painted Glass**

There is very little ancient painted glass to-day in the churches of the City of London, and such of it as there is is mainly heraldic glass of the 17th century. As to the medieval glass which filled the windows of the ancient churches, religious fanaticism of the 16th and 17th centuries, neglect of the 18th and early 19th centuries and the Great Fire of 1666 together disposed of most of it. Modern restorers and collectors have done the rest. Here and there a few fragments of early glass remain, such as those in a west window of St. Katherine Cree Church.

Chitty

The Church of All Hallows Barking is no exception to this state of things ; all the painted glass there, which can be called ancient, is heraldic glass of the 17th century. It seems likely that it is assignable to the year 1666, although only two panels bear that date, and that it was intended as a memorial of the devastating fire of that year. Beginning with the South Aisle, the first window from the east contains a late heater-shaped shield bearing a red cross (pot-metal) in a silver field. The field has a floral diaper and there is no sign of there having been a red sword in the first quarter ; it is probable that either the sword originally there has decayed or that the quarter containing it has been broken and lost, and a modern restoration without the sword has been inserted in its place ; there can be little doubt that this shield was intended to bear the arms of the City of London and was originally the central part of a full Achievement-of-arms, crested and mantled helm and supporters.

In the second window from the east is an oblong panel, painted in enamel colours, containing a late heater-shaped shield, much broken and repaired with lead, bearing *azure on a bend cotised argent 3 martlets gules, on the helm, mantled gules, doubled argent, the crest, a talbot's head proper issuing*

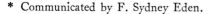

* Communicated by F. Sydney Eden.

from a coronet or. The blue-enamel field of the shield has almost entirely perished and the mantling is very fragmentary, having disappeared from the sides of the shield and white glass inserted in its place. Below the shield, on a yellow stain label, is the date 1666: the label is set in a blue enamel ground much decayed, with yellow scroll work and border.

In Papworth's Ordinary these arms are assigned to Edwards of London, and also to the name of Southhouse.

An oblong panel is in the fourth window from the east. Viewed from the floor level, it gives the general impression of white and yellow and green: when closely examined, it is found to be made up of fragments. In the centre is a shield with a modern white-glass field, though there is a minute piece of blue glass in the dexter side of it: in this field is a yellow cheveron, separately leaded. The shield is set in fragmentary scrollwork and leafage — a pomegranate below the shield, a shell above it, and a piece of modern dark blue glass between the shell and the shield. It is impossible to say whether the shield is meant for a partial restoration of an actual coat-of-arms or is merely a putting-together of fragments in heraldic form.

In the fifth window from the east is a very fragmentary piece which was formerly in the third window. In consists of a piece of modern white glass cut into the shape of a very debased pattern of shield and set in fragments, among them several small pieces of yellow glass bearing Renaissance scrollwork, probably from a lost heraldic design.

The North Aisle contains only one piece of old painted glass—in the second window from the east. It consists of a panel, similar in size and style to that in the corresponding window in the South Aisle, and shows a shield bearing *argent on a bend azure 3 square buckles or; on the helm, mantled gules doubled argent, the crest, on a wreath argent and azure a hand couped at the wrist rising from clouds proper holding an estoile or.* At foot of the panel is a yellow label, set in yellow and coloured scrolled border, with the inscription:

Glassed
ab Incarnatione A fatali 1666
conflagrationis Londini

On the bottom line of the yellow border of this panel are scratched the following names, *W. Warde April 3, John Fishe Arble* (April) 9 1789.

There are scratchings similar to these on the panel in the second window from the east in the South Aisle—*Henry White, George Jend . . .* and *G. Price . . . church in . . . window.* These scratchings tell of the time when the windows were accessible to scribblers by reason of galleries in the aisles.

As Papworth assigns the arms in this panel to the name of Starling, they are, no doubt, meant to refer to Sir Samuel Starling (or Sterlinge) who was Lord Mayor in 1669, and, according to Beaven's *Aldermen of London,* was knighted in 1667, was Alderman of Vintry Ward in 1661 and belonged to the Companies of Brewers and Drapers. Sir Samuel died in 1674.

66

APPENDIX I

FORTY DAYS' INDULGENCE TO THOSE WHO PAY DEVOTIONS IN THE CHAPEL IN THE CHURCHYARD OF BERKYNGCHIRCHE

Universis sancte matris ecclesie filiis, presentes literas inspecturis Nos miseracione divina . . . [Johannes] Ciuitatis Noue Johannes Carpenteran' Adrianus, Tartarorum Episcopi, & domini Pape legati, salutem in domino sempiternam. Quia datum est nobis intelligi per illustrissimum Regem Anglie, Edwardum filium Regis Henrici quod capella in cimiterio de Berkyngchirche, London' situata per strenuum Ricardum quondam Regem Anglie [mi]rabiliter extiterat fundata Ac eciam qualiter Wallences Angliam inuaserunt viuente dicto Henrico & patriam undique devastauerunt homines ac mulieres ac infantes in Cunabulis occiderunt & quod auditu horrendum est mulieres in puerperio decubantes gladio trucidauerunt & ulterius Insulam de Ely hostiliter ceperunt & illam per vnum annum manu forti custodierunt, & finaliter indempnes cum tempus sibi placuerit Walliam redierunt Idem Edwardus tunc temporis juvenis tot dampna cernens Inurias & obprobria in exheredicionem patris sui & destruccionem totius Anglie fleuit amariter ac tantam doloris tristiciam acerbi cordisque merorem presertim suo corpori ministrauit vt lecto recumbens penitus semiuiuo relicto nullam se credidit totaliter sanitatem recuperare Quadam vero nocte dei genitricis marie auxilium postulans piam ejus clemenciam deuote implorauit vt ipsum ex diuina reuelacione nocturna visione inspiraret quomodo de Wallensibus Anglici possent citissime vindicari. Vt factum est autem eo dormiente virgo venustissima omnium virtutum floribus insignita virgo dei genitrix gloriosa cujus precibus iuuatur populus Christianus florem inmarcessibilem & eternum ineffabili sancti Spiritus cooperacione produxit, quasi nocturna visione ipsi apparuit dicens O Edwarde amice dei quid clamas Ecce assum Scias pro certo quod viuente patre tuo non possunt Wallenses ab anglicis totaliter opprimi aut subiugari & hoc est ob patris tui vile peccatum ac nimias extorciones. Sed vade cras mane ad quendam Judeum nomine Marlibrunum totius mundi sapienciorem picture artificem apud Billingesgate London' commorantem, & eum tibi facere ymaginem constringas sub tali forma qua modo me vides qui ex diuina inspiracione duas in ipsa perficiet facies unam filio meo Jesu valde similem alteram mihi in cunctis consimilem perornabit, vt nulla difformitas possit ab aliquo veraciter enarrari Ipsam ymaginem sic plene compositam Capelle in Cimiterio de Berkyngchirche iuxta turrim London' situate quamtocius destinare studeas & ibidem ex parte aquilonari decenter ornari facias vnde maiora tibi mirabilia scias veraciter protinus eminere Nam tam cito quam facierum vultus dictus Mar[l]ibrunus infra ipsam Capellam diligenter inspexerit mox in amorem celestem affectabitur vt ad fidem catholicam unacum vxore sua Juda conuertetur qui postmodum tibi multa Judorum secreta est reuelaturus vnde puniendi sunt   Et tu, Edwarde, cum hoc

67

miraculum videris omnipotenti deo votum tuum voue quod te viuente & in Anglia existente quolibet anno quinquies dictam ymaginem sub honore matris Christi visitabis, eandemque Capellam quociescunque opus fuerit reparabis, & sustentabio Nam ille locus vere est laudandus qui cum hoc votum genuflectendo feceris & iuxta tuum posse firmiter impleueris vbicumque in mundo fueris super omnes gentes semper victoriosissimus atque insuperabilis eris & mortuo patre tuo tu es Rex Anglie subjugator Wallie & oppressor tocius scocie futurus Insuper crede michi quod quilibet iustus Anglie monachus seu forte alius qui hoc votum deuote vouerit & iuxta suum posse firmiter adimpleuerit super Wallenses & scotos semper sine dubio victoriosissimus atque insuperabilis erit Et hiis dictis euanuit Vt ergo euigilans, & sui sompnum commemorauit velut raptus pene spiritu cepit admirari. Verum tamen totum impleuit quemadmodum per sompnum in mandatis prehabuit Insuper coram nobis in presentia multorum magnatum tam Anglie quam scocie dictus Edwardus sponte prestitit juramentum quod omnia per sompnum sibi ostensa ut predictum est hucusque inuenit verissima Nos igitur cupientes ut dicta Capella congruis honoribus frequentetur & a Christi fidelibus iugiter veneretur omnibus vere penitentibus et confessis qui ad ipsam Capellam causa devocionis et oracionis accesserint & qui ad luminaria reparamenta ac ornamenta manus suas porrexerint adiutrices necnon & qui pro animabus nobilis Ricardi quondam Regis Anglie cuius cor in eadem Capella sub summo altari requiescit humatum Et omnium fidelium defunctorum in Christo quiescencium oracionem dominicam cum salutacione Angelica quociescunque & quandocunque pia mente dixerint de omnipotentis dei misericordia & beatorum Petri & Pauli Apostolorum eius meritis & auctoritate confisi singuli singulas quadragenas dierum de Inunctis eis penitenciis misericorditer in domino relaxamus dum tamen loci diocesanus hanc nostram ratam habuerit Indulgenciam. In quorum omnium testimonium presentes literas nostris sigillis duximus roborandas. Data apud Northam existente Parliamento tam Anglie quam scocie vicesimo die Maii Anno Domini Millesimo Ducentesimo nonagesimo brimo [sic].

The text as here printed occurs in London Episc. Reg., Gilbert, f. 194, and differs considerably from the version printed by Newcourt (*Repertorium* App.). The marginal notes, in a hand which added notes throughout the register read : (*a*) Nota quomodo Wallenses Inuaserunt Regnum et que dampna inde peruaeniebant et quomodo tandem ex Reuelacione Diuin[a] Virginis Marie facta Edwardo Regi Anglie vindicabantur; and (*b*) In hiis litteris continetur de factura ymag[inis] s[ancte] marie in ca[pella] iux[t]a Berkyn[g]chirch.

The Register itself is that of Bishop Gilbert, who was Bishop of London, 1436 to 1448. The indulgence occurs directly after an imperfect Act on the same folio relating to an agreement between a Bishop of London and the Prior and Chapter of Christchurch, Canterbury, the See of Canterbury being vacant, and among a number of miscellanea relating to Thele, Steple, and Canterbury, and occupying folios 192 to 194. The Register is not in the same hand throughout.   At f. 203 follows a similar Indulgence for Edmonton parish church entered as this one is without any letters of inspection or confirmation, but in the hand of the clerk who wrote the bulk of the Register.   It is clear that these Indulgences were either entered at the end of Gilbert's episcopate, or after his death (July 1448); but neither is in the hand which at f. 207 begins the Register of Walter Sherington clerk Canon of St. Paul's, official and *Custos* of the Spiritualities upon the death of Gilbert.

The whole register was bound in 1529.*

* I am much indebted to Miss Minnie Reddan for very generous help in respect to this and other records relating to the history of the church.—L. J. R.

APPENDIX II

INVENTORY OF CHURCH GOODS IN 1452

This endenture made the xvj. day of October The yere of Our Lord. mcccclij. and the yere of the regne of Kyng Henry sixte. xxxj^{ti}. betwene John Ereth John Wyllaston and Robert Caterton wardeynes of the goodes of the chirche of Alhalowen Berkyng of London on that oon partie, and John Hobbes and William Payn clerkes of the saide chirche on that other partie. witnesseth That the seid John Hobbes and William Payn clerkes knowelech and graunten him by this present endenture to have receyued of the seide wardeynes the forseid. xvj. day October in the seide chirche the goodes and ornamentes after writen and perteynyng to the seide chirche the which goodes and ornamentes the foreseid clerkes shall sikerly and saufly kepe withynne the same chirche to the vse and profit there off as long as they there shall continue in seruice so that what tyme here after it happe the seid John and William clerkes to be duly warned by the seid wardeynes or her successoures wardeynes of the forseid chirche for the tyme beyng. to yelde and deliuere the same goodes and ornamentes to the forseid wardeynes or her successors that thanne the seid clerkes shall make deliuerance of the same goodes and ornamentes frely without any delay.

> First .ij. good newe masse bokes.
> Item .ij. olde masse bokes.
> Item .j. masse boke lent to the chapell.
> Item .iij. grayelles newe.
> Item .ij. grayelles olde not Sales b[er]y.
> Item .j. antiphonere newe.
> Item .ij. olde antiphoners of olde Salesbery vse.
> Item j antiphonere newe with all his legendes.
> Item .j. boke for the dexte for principall dayes for matens.
> Item .j. collectary boke.
> Item .j. venite boke.
> Item .j. boke with ympnes noted.
> Item .ij. legendes *Temporum et Sanctorum* newe.
> Item j Epistolary boke newe bounden.
> Item .ij. processionaries.
> Item .j. processionarie and .j. manuell bounden to geder.
> Item a good newe manuell.
> Item j ordinall boke.
> Item another ordinall in quayers of the yifte of John Mason.
> Item .ij. sauters covered with rede lether.
> Item .j. boke cheyned in the quere called Pupilla.
> Item .ij. quaieres of the story of seint Anne.

Item a resurreccion of siluer and ouergilt with a birell for the sacrament weying of troye weght .iiij lb. vj. vnces.
> Item j coupe of siluer for the sacrement weying of troye xvj vnces.

70

Item a crismatorie of siluer weying largely xvj vnces and more.

Item j. senser of siluer weying .iij. lb. ij. vnces dj troye.

Item .ij. basyns of siluer weying .iiij. lb. xj vnces dj. tr[oy]e.

Item .j. shippe of siluer with a spone .x. vnces dj q[uar]t[er] tr[oy]e.

Item .ij. candelstikkes of siluer .j. lb. ij unces. iij. q[uar]t[ers].

Item .j. crosse of siluer enameled w^t the fote of siluer weying .v. lb. ij vnces, di tree and all with ynne.

Item .j crosse plated with siluer and the fote of coper weying in all w^t ye tree wyth ynne. iiij. lb. viij vnces. tro[ye].

Item .j pix for the sacrement hangying in the canopee aboue the high auter weying .vj. vnces tro[ye].

Item .j. grete chalys siluer and ouergilt called Knolles chalys. iiij. lb. iij. vnces dj.

Item .j. chalys marked w^t a l[ett]re of A. weying j. lb. tro[ye].

Item j chalys w^t. B. ix vnces. di.

Item .j. chalys w^t. C. xi vnces. iij q[uar]t[ers].

Item j. chalys w^t D. j. lb. iij q[uar]t[ers].

Item j. chalys w^t E. j. lb. j. vnce dj and dj q[uar]t[er].

Item j. chalys w^t F. of the yifte of Thomas Attemille .j. lb. v. vnces. j. q[uar]t[er].

Item a chalys w^t G. x vnces. iij. q[uar]t[ers]. dj.

Item .j. chalys w^t H. .j. lb. scarse.

Item a senser of coper and ouergilt.

Item .j. crosse of coper and ouergilt.

Item .ij. crosse shaftes peynted that on w^t gold and that other w^t siluer.

Item .ij. standard candelstikkes of laton before the high auter.

Item j. myddel peire candelstikkes of laton for weddynges.

Item iij lasse peire candelstikkes of laton for small tapers.

Item j candelstik of laton marked w^t an hewet.

Item j candelstik of laton w^t a nose for morowe masse.

Item .ij. halywater stoppes of laton w^t a sprynkell of laton.

Item .vj. cruettes of pewter.

Item .j. potell pot of pewter for lampe oyle.

Item an hole sute of vestimentes of blak and grene w^t iij. copes sewyinge.

Item j. sute of rede cloth of gold that is to saye : chesible ij. tunicles .iij. aubes iij. amytes with the stoles and fanons and .j. cope of the same sute.

Item j vestiment of blu baudekyn the ground p[ur]pill w^t blu libardes for preest deken and subdeken.

Item j. vestiment of grene that is to seye : j chesible .j. awbe and ij. tunicles.

Item .j. singell vestiment hole for the preest of blak silk.

Item .j. singell vestiment of white silk w^t a crucifix be hynde in the chesibill.

Item j. singell vestiment of blu baudekyn w^t j olde cope of the same sute.

Item .j. vestiment of grene baudekyn and ij tunicles of the same sute.

Item j. feriall vestiment of grene veluet striped w^t rede.

Item j. feriall vestiment of russet w^t lyons rampand.

Item j. feriall vestiment of olde cloth of gold the ground grene.

Item j. singell vestiment of rede and grene w^t lyons of gold.

Item .j. vestiment of baudekyn the grounde p[ur]pil w^t roses and blue cranes.

Item .j. singell vestiment of olde clothe of golde rede.

Item j singell vestiment of rede for Good Friday.

Item j singell vestiment for the preest of white bustian w^t .j. cope and .ij. tunicles of the same.

*Item a singell vestiment of blak worsted.

Item j singell vestiment of russet damask longyng to the auter of seint Steph[e]n.

Item to the same auter another vestiment of blu baudekyn w^t an hewet in the parure.

Item j. vestiment of white fustian for lenten.

Item j. ferial vestiment of white russet rayed for lenten.

Item j cope of rede silk w^t lyons of gold.

Item .j. cope of white cloth of gold.

Item .j. cope of rede veluet embrouded w^t conduytes.

Item .j. cope of blak silk old and perused

Item .ij. litell copes of grene for children.

Item .ij. clothes of gold of the gifte of the galymen.

†Item parures of cloth of gold for an awbe and an amyte.

Item for the high auter aboue and benethe that is to seye; front and contrefront of rede satyn w^t .j. frontell of rede cloth of gold and ij. curtynes of rede tartaryn.

Item for the same auter front and contrefr[ont] of white tartaryn pouderd w^t blu garters and j frontell of the same w^t .ij. curtynes of white tartaryn.

Item to the same auter front and contrefront of rede cloth of gold w^t a frontell of grene silk.

Item for the same auter front and contre[front] of blu steyned w^t ij. curtynes steyned w^t angels.

Item .iiij. towelles for the same auter conteynyng euery pece .iiij. elles in lengthe.

Item .iiij. towelles sewed vppon the frontels euery pece cont[eynyng] .iiij. elles.

Item j olde autercloth of the same lengthe.

Item .j. olde frontel of blu silk for the high auter.

* Interlined above; this was bequeathed by Tylling in 1458.
† Underlined.

72

Item .j. olde frontel of silk for the same auter grene yelowe and rede.

Item for our lady auter a countrefrount of tartaryn grene and white w^t .ij. curteyns of the same and j frontell of blu silk w^t j towell sowed therto.

Item to the Trinitee auter .j front and contre[front] of white steyned w^t briddes of gold w^t .ij. curtyns steyned.

Item for the small auters .v. frontelles of diuerse sortes that is to seye; one w^t bokels of gold steyned / Another of blu steyned w^t roses of gold Another of grene and rede w^t floures of gold the iiij^e of white cloth of gold and the v. w^t apostels hedes steyned.

Item .ij. curteyns of grene steyned w^t angels and white roses.

Item .ij. cúrteyns of grene steyned w^t a W crowned and a marchantes mark.

Item for the high auter one olde steyned cloth of blu.

Item for seint Steph[e]n auter front contrefr[ont] and frontell of silk raies white w^t garters and ij curtynes of silk.

Item to the same auter front and ij curtynes steyned white and al aboue ij clothes steyned oon grene and another white.

Item for the same auter ij frontes j. contrefr[ont] and ij curtynes of white steyned w^t the passion for lenten.

Item iij olde countrefrontes of diuerse sortes steyned for small auters.

Item for lente .j. veill of white lynnen cloth and xvij peces grete and smale for the auters and to hele the ymages in lenten tyme.

Item of cloth steyned w^t the passion for the rode in lenten.

Item of longe cloth steyned hangyng before the rode lofte.

Item j blak cloth of silk longyng to the lampe light for pore men.

Item .iiij. olde steyned clothes that is to seye; one w^t the salutacion of our lady. Another w^t the ymages of seynt John Baptist and seynt Petre/ and ij other w^t roses of gold. / And j curtyne of grene w^t roses of gold.

Item vij auterclothes good and badde to ley vppon the smale auters of lynnen cloth.

Item .j. longe towell for houselyng on Esterday cont[aining] xiij elles large.

Item j other towell cont[aining] in lengthe vj elles di. large.

Item j towell cont[aining] v. elles.

Item j towell cont[aining] .iij. elles.

Item j towell cont[aining] .iiij. elles.

Item .iiij. smale towels.

Item j olde veill of blu and yelowe.

Item j cloth of blu tapesserie to lye a fore the high auter.

Item ij olde steyned clothes / j. olde cope of white p[er]used / and iij. olde frontels for the small auters p[er]used.

Item ij longe ridels of blue steyned and rynged for both sides of the quere.

Item for the sepulcre ij longe peces of blu velewet embrouded w^t sterres of gold of cipres / iiij quarters and .ij. smale peces of the same sute / and .ij. clothes hangers of blue tartaryn w^t sterres of gold.

G

Item iiij kerchiefs of plesaunce for the same.

Item j celo^r steyned with the Trinitee for the sepulcre.

Item .x. corporasses w^t casses and j casse voide.

Item .xij. pilowes of silk.

Item .iij kerchiefs of lawne fyne ech of an hole plice of the yifte of dame Margerie Haydok.

Item .j. banner of white tartaryn newe w^t an ymage of oure lady.

Item .j. pynnon of tartaryn w^t a rede lyon.

Item .iiij. baners of silk of diuerse sortes.

Item .xvij. baners olde of diuerse sortes.

Item xij pensels of Ostritch feders.

Item .j. miter for seynt Nicholas bisshop.

Item .ij. newe surplys and .ij. olde surplys.

Item .j. superaltare of marbell.

Item .j. litel iron panne to fetch fyre.

Item .j. spruce cheste bound w^t yron.

Item .ij. longe coffres in the chauncill and j longe coffre in the chirch be nethe to fore our lady auter for torches.

Item iiij newe torches and .iij. other good torches litel worn or spended.

Item .j. ladder of .xxvij. ronges.

And it is accorded betwene the seid parties that in cas that any of the seid goodes or ornamentes be aliened or lost in defaute of the seid clerkes they abidying in office w^t ynne the seide chirche; that thanne the seide clerkes graunten by this present endenture to paye and content resonably for thoo goodes and ornamentes so in her defaut aliened or lost.

In witness of the which thing to these present endentures the parties aboueseid eche to other have put to her seles And for more seurtee on the party of the seid William Payn clerk of all couenantes above writen on his party well and truly to be performed Simond Strete citesein and groser of London to this present endenture hath sette to his seel Yeuen at London in the parissh aboueseid the day and yere aboue writen.

[Added in another hand.]

Item a manuell w^t a colectory the gyfte off sir Thom[as] Vyrlry* late vycary / w^t ij surplyses slevyd to the vse of the qwere and a lytell autercloth of grene tartron w^t rayes wyith and blak.

[On a smaller piece of vellum attached.]

The newe missall with the claspes of siluer and gilt—of the yifte of Nicholl Brymmesgrove sumtyme vicare of Berkyng.

Another good missall newe—of the yifte of dame Margery Welton.

Item a Resureccion of siluer and gilt—of the yifte of the seid dame Margery.

Item a crismatory of silver—of the yifte of the seid dame Margery.

* [*Sic*], in error for " Vyrby."

74

Item a pix of siluer hangyng in the canopee—of the yifte of the seid dame Margery.

Item a front of rede cloth of gold for the high auter embrouded w^t the Trinitee—of the yifte of the seid dame Margery.

Item ij candelstikkes of siluer of the yifte of the Galymen.

Item the crosse plated with siluer and the fote of coper—of the yifte of the Galymen.

Item ij chalys marked vppon the patyns that oon w^t B and th^t other with D—— of the yifte of the Galymen.

Item an hole sute of vestimentes blak and grene—of the yifte of Symkyn Hugh.

Item the sute of rede cloth of gold—of the yifte of Sir Robert Knolles knyght.

Item j singell vestiment of blak worsted—of the yifte of Sir William Tillyng chauntry preest.

Item the frount countrefrount of rede satyn and ij curtynes of rede tartaryn for the high auter—of the yifte of John Pontrell.

Item j frount and countrefrount of white tartaryn w^t garters and ij curtyns of white tartaryn for the high auter of the yifte of .J. Croke.

Item j baner of white tartaryn w^t an ymage of our lady—of the yifte of the Galymen.

Endorsed

No 1   A deed from the clergy to the church wardens concerning the ornaments mass books etc belonging to the church dated 16th October 1452.

APPENDIX III

INVENTORY OF CHURCH GOODS, 1506

Jhesus. the xxx daye of Juyne A[nn]o xvCvj.

The daye above reherssyd the holl[e] p[ar]ysche of all Hallowe barkynge mad the vewe of the chyrche goodes as here after Ensuythe bye the partyculer parcelles of all maner ornementtes.

Emprimis iij Copys wythe the prest and ij de[cu]nse of red cloythe off tyseewe.

Item iij Copys w^t the prest and ij Dekons of blewe welwett wythe Rossys

ij Copys wythe prest and ij dekens of blew wellwet wythe sterys

j Cope wythe prest deken and s[u]bdekene off Red bawdkyne

iij Copys prest deken and s[u]bdekene off wheyt bustyan powdyrd wythe garters

j Cope prest deken and s[u]bdeken of blewe sylke powderd wythe essys and bestes

j Cope prest deken and s[u]bdeken of blake damaske pleyne

ij old copys of blake wythe brawnchys of grene sylke wythe prest deken and s[u]bdeken

j Cope of wheyght bustyan for seynt nycholaz powderd wythe gartersse wythe A gowne and A hod of Red cloythe

ij myterse the one wythe Rossys & the othyr steryse

j Cope wythe prest dekone and s[u]bdeken of wheyght bawkyne powdyrd wythe syke and gold

j vestementt of gren chamlett of Metfordes geft

j Corporas Case of blake & grene & the Corporas in ytt

j vestementt of wheyght bawdkyne powdyrd w^t byrdes

j Cope of wheyght bawdkyne powdyrd wythe Red and grene

j vestmentt of Red bawdkyne w^t crownes and bestes

j Cope of wheyghtt damaske powdyrd wythe essys of gold the orferase of ymages

j Cope of Red bawdkyne powdyrd wythe pellykane

j Cope of tawnye Damaske old the orferase Conyse and howndes

j Red vestement of worsted w^t emyse

j vestement of purpyle wellwett

ij chyldyrnesse Copys of grene bavdkyne

j red Cope old wythe bestes of gold powdyrd

ij Corperase Cassys of good nedle warke one w^t bestes and the othyr wythe byrdes

j Jewell of crystall hollow wythe iiij fett and one Agglott of sylver and gylt

j vestement off [wheygh grene]* blake fustyan of naplles w^t A Crose of red wellwett

* Erased.

76

j awtyrclothe of Red satan one benethe & Anothyr Aboofe wythe frontyle of Red bawdkyne and ij Corteynz of chonghabyle sarsenet

j awtyr cloythe of blewe sarsenet one benethe and Anothyr Aboofe powdyrd wythe sterrys and A frontyll to the same w^t ij Corteynse

j awtyr cloythe of wheyght sarsenet one for benethe & Anothyr Abovfe w^t front & ij Cortense to the same powdyrd wythe garters

j awtyr cloythe for Abovfe and beneythe of gren bavdkyne w^t All-hallowe there on

j red awtyre cloythe payntyd for benethe of spryngs gyft

j awtyr cloythe of dyapre markyd letters of sylke

j* awtyre cloythese w^t Corteynz for all iij awterse for the terme of lentt

j awtyr cloyth of blake worsted w^t A crucyfyxe one Abovfe and Anothyr benethe w^t ij Cortenz of blake sarcenet

j awtyr cloythe of [seynt katerynz]† the trinyte w^t seynt kateryn & seynt margerte & A frontyle off sylke powdyrd w^t branchys and ij Cor-teynse of leynyn cloythe steyned

j Awtyr cloythe of wheyght and grene w^t a front of bavdkyne and ij Corteynse of byrds eyne

j Awtyr cloythe of dyapur wythe A frontt of wheyght damaske of Master Metfordes gyft

j Awtyr cloythe of dyapur cont[aining] v yerdes of the gyft of John Dyxe and ell brod

j Awtyr cloythe of dyapur of thomas rychrdsonz gyft cont[aining] v yerdes‡ and of yerd brod

j Awtyr cloythe of dyapur markyd w^t A croyse of red and thornis there Abowght cont[aining] iiij yerdes

ij verye old cloythse of Damaske brokyne

---

* Altered from " ij."
† Erased.
‡ Altered from " elles."

APPENDIX IV

INVENTORY OF THE CHURCH GOODS, 1512

This endenture mayd the xx daye of Maye the ȝere of hower lord M'CCCCC and xij and the ȝere of the reygne of kynge Harry the viij^te iiij betwenne mayster William Gedyng vicker William Welbeck and William Aschewell wayrdens of the chyrche of Alhallon Barkyng of London on that ton partte and Rychard Gryffen and Edmond Sargonsces clerkes of the sayd chyrche on the other partte wytnessytth that the sayd Rychard and Edmond clerkes knolege and gravnten them by thys pressent endenturs to haue re[ceived] of the bove sayd wardens the day a bove wryttyn all soche gooddes and ornamentes belongeng to the bove sayd chyrche as here aft^r ys wryttyn the wyche gooddes and ornamentes the forsayd clerkes schall sykerly and saffely kepe w^t in the same chyrche to the vsse and proffet there of as longe as they there schall contynowe in servysse so that wat tyme hereaft^r yt appe the sayd Rycharde and Edmond clerkes to be dowlly warned by the sayd wayrdens or here successors wayrdens of the for sayd chyrche for the tyme being to yelde and delijuer the same gooddes and ornamentes to the for sayd wardens or here successors wardens that than the sayd clerkes schall mayke delyuerans of the same gooddes and ornamentes frely w^t owt anny deley / And it ys agreed betwenne the sayd parttes that in casse that anny of the sayd gooddes or ornamentes be alyened or loyst in deffowte of the sayd clarkes they abydying in offysse w^t in the sayd chyrche that than the sayd clerkes granten by thes pressent endenturs to pay and content resonably for thoo gooddes or ornamentes so in there deffawte alyned or loyst In wetnes of the wyche thynge to thes pressent endenturs the parttes a bove sayd eche to other haue putto there selles and for more surtey on the partte of the sayd Rychard Gryffen clerke of all conavntes above wryttyn on hys partte well and trully to be performed William Dennam citesyn and yremong^r of London and Robert Mayssey citesyn and tawȝeer of London have putto there selles and in lyche wysse on the partte of Edmond Sargonsces Nycolas Gennyns cetesyn and skynner of London and William Stonne citesyn and Fuller of London have puttoe there selles the day and jere a bove wryttyn.

PLATTE AND JOWELLES

Item ij bayssons of syluer parssell gyltte w^t on w^t the red rosses and the other w^t a red crosse in the myddys of the bayssons weying
lix onces iij q^rt^rs di

Item a monster of syluer and gylte for the sacrament pȝ   vij^xx onces di

Item a sensser of syluer parssell gyltte pȝ   xxxij onces

Item another of the same lyche pȝ   xxxij onces

Item a schyppe of syluer parssell gylte pȝ   x onces on qrtr

Item ij candelstyches of syluer pȝ   xv onces

Item ar esurieccion w^t a tombe. i croysse and a scryne all syluer and gyltte   liii onces di

Item ij cruettes of syluer pȝ w^t a smalle crose   x onces

78

Item a nell of syluer weying   viij onces
Item a paxe of syluer and gyltte w^t a crownne p$_3$ iiij onces di di qrt^r
Item a paxe of syluer and gylte blew ennamylet p$_3$ vj onces
Item a jewell of byrall weying   iij onces
Item a crysmatory of syluer parssell gylte p$_3$ xviij onces
Item a pyxe of syluer with a pesse of syluer there in and a crosse thereapon syluer and gylte with Mary and John p$_3$ xvij onces di
Item the beyst crosse of syluer and gyltte w^t Mary and John p$_3$
                                      lxij onces

Item a crosse of syluer and gylte with a pyn of yron p$_3$ iiij^{xx} iiij onces.

Item a rownd baylle of syluer and gylte for the sacrament p$_3$ xxj onces.

Item a crosse of tymber plattyd with syluer and the crosse thereupon syluer and gylte.

Item the beyst challes with the patent syluer and gylte p$_3$ lj onces di.

Item a challys with the pattent of syluer p$_3$ xix onces iij quarters.

Item a challys parssell gylte with the pattent with the armes of the whytte crosse and a barre of gold goying ouer p$_3$ xvij onces.

Item a challis parssell gyltte w^t y^e pattent & Jesus hed there apon p$_3$ xiiij onces.

     a nother of the same merke p$_3$ ix onces.
     a nother of the same merke p$_3$ xiij onces.
     another of the same merke p$_3$ xij onces.
     a challis . . . gylte w^t y^e pattent and a lambe the[re ap]on p$_3$ xij onces. dim.
     ij gret [candle]stikes offe [*sic*].
     ij croches [for] the Rector corys [*sic*] of sillver w^t Red stavys.
     ij coppys of whytt damask w^t jes & Kays of gold w^t the orferas of Red clothe of gold.
     prest dekon subdekon of whytt damask w^t Js & Kayis.
     a vestment w^t dekon & subdekon of black silk branchyd w^t gren.

CORPORASSES W^T CASSES

Item the beyst corporas w^t a Caas of popynjays of nedyll worke.
     a Corporas of gold & nedyl worke w^t beystis & ffowles & armes.
     a Corporas of gold a boytth syddys.
     a Corporas w^t sent Kateryn a pon hyt.
     ij old corporas w^t lyons of gold a pon them.
     a Corporas of Crymsyn damaske and grenne sarssenet.
     a Corporas of gold and bavdekyn.
     a Corporas of grenne and crymsyn vellvet.
     ij corporas more vnchargid.

VESTMENTIS

Item a sutte w iij Coppys of gold a pon blacke velvet.
     a sutte w^t iij Coppys of gold a pon Red velvet.

Item a sutte wᵗ iij Coppys of blewe velvet wᵗ wytte Rosses.
a sutte wᵗ iij Coppys of blewe velvet wᵗ steerys.
a sutte wᵗ on coppe of whytte sylke wᵗ branches of gold.
a sutte wᵗ on coppe of Red bavdekyn.
a sutte wᵗ iij coppys of bustyan whytte gartters.
[a sutte wᵗ iij Coppys of blacke sylke branchyd wᵗ grenne]*
a sutte off Coppys blacke [damaske]* brugis satten.
a sutte wᵗ on Coppe of blewe sylke wᵗ dyuers workis.
a vestment of purpull velvet.
a vestment of greyne chamlet.
a vestment of Red wᵗ Jesus a pon hyt.
a Coppe of wytte damaske wᵗ esses.
[a Coppe of whellis].*
a Coppe of whytte bavdekyn for sent nycolas.
a gownne & a hewd of Red belongeng yᵉ same.

BOOKES

Item iij maysse bookes & a pystell pooke wᵗ iij antyphyners.
ij old antyphyners & ij ymners & (ij wrytton)† iiij manualis pryntid.
a Collectre & v. grayelles & vij prosessiners v[ery] [perichenge.
ij legendis on of the temporallis & a nother of Sanctorum [vj prented].†
a Respysary wᵗ a [dorge bowcke].*   Another legend pryntid.
a nolde peresheng savter.*   A nold ordineryt, A nother legend pryntid†.

SEPOWLKER CLOTTHES & BANNERS

Item. ij sepulker cloytthes of blewe sarssynet wᵗ noli me tangere.
xij pendantes of Red bokeram & ij longe standerdis of Red bokeram wᵗ ij syluer lyons & a square banner of bokeram wᵗ the Kyngis armes & xii square banners and pendantis.
iiij banner cloytthes for crossys & a good banner cloytth of the trynete of sylke.
viij pecis of blew welvett wᵗ starrys of gold.
a havtter cloth of above & beneth panyd wᵗ Red (& grene cloth)‡ of gold and a havlter passe of the same wᵗ ij curtens of sursenet of Red and grene.

* Erased.
† Interlineated.
‡ Interlineated and " cloth of the same " erased.

THE PARISH OF ALL HALLOWS BARKING

THE HYGHT AVTER CLOTTHES

Item a havtter clotthe above & be netthe of Red satten.

a ffrontell of Red bavdekyn w^t ij covrtens Red sylke.

a avtter chotth a bove & benetth of blewe sarssenet powdert w^t sterrys & a ffrontell w^t ij cowrtens of ye same.

for a bove & beneytth of greynne bavdekyn w^t alhallon brodered & a frontell w^t ij courtens of ye same.

for a bove & be neyth of whytte sarssenet powdert w^t garters in the vpper cloytth.

ffor a bove & beynetth for leynt of steynyd worke w^t ij cowrtens of the same.

a Cloytth of the trynyte.

a greynne cowrtten of sarsenet w^t strypys.

SEYNT NYCOLAS AVTER

Item a avtter Cloytthe ffor a bove & be neytth of blacke worsted w^t a crusyfyxe & mary & John and ij cowrtens of blacke sarsynet.

a cloytth ffor leynt a bove & beneyth w^t red crossys.

(a vnder cloytth w^t estryge ffeythers)* steyned.

a cloytth steynyd w^t sent grygorys petty w^t ij cowrtens of scheker sylke on hallffe brent.

TRYNYTE AUTER

Item a Cloytth of the trynete w^t sent Kateryn & sent marget a ffrontell of sylke powdert w^t branches & ij cowrtens of lynnen cloyth steyned.

SEYNTE THOMAS & HOWER LADYS AVTER

Item a Cloytth for leynt & a ffrontell of whyte damaske brodered w^t angelles of gold & a cloytth of lynnen steynyd w^t deus miseriatur nostri (& a cloytth vnder of the hart of Jesus)* & a ffrontel of bavdekyn w^t sterrys & fflowers & ij cowrtens Red sylke & ij cowrtens steynyd w^t angelles.

SEYNT ANNYS AVTER

Item a cloyth whytte & greynne partte (w^t a ffrontell)* of bavdekyn (w^t ij cowrtens whytte & greynne)*.

a cloytthe w^t a ffrontell of blewe bavdekyn & a cowrten of whytte for the vpper partte for lent.

Item ffor a bove & be neytthe of wytte sarsenet w^t garters.

* Erased.

AVTER CLOTHES OF DYAPER

Item a avtter cloytth of dyaper w^t a pesse lynnen cloyth cont[aining] iiii helles.

a cloytth of dyaper w^t ye name of Robert schester cont[aining] iiij helles dim.

a cloytth of dyaper w^t ij blew crosses cont[aining] iij helles dim.

a cloytth of dyaper ij ʒardes brod w^t iij Red crosses cont[aining] iij helles.

a cloytth of dyaper ij ʒardes brod w^t owt mark cont[aining] iiij helles iij quarters.

a cloytth of dyaper cont[aining] iiij helles another ard—iiij helles.

a cloytth of dyaper w^t v blew strypys cont[aining] iiij helles quarter.

a Cloyth of dyaper cont[aining] iiij helles dim. another cont[aining] v. helles dim.

a Cloytth of dyper w^t lylley p[ott]es cont[aining] iij helles dim.

a Cloytth of dyaper cont[aining] iij helles iij quarters a nother cont[aining] iij helles iij quarters.

a cloytth of dyaper w^t a Red crosse cont[aining] iij helles dim.

a cloytth of dyaper cont[aining] ij helles another cont[aining] iiij helles.

a cloytth playnne w^t blewe strypys cont[aining] iij helles.

a cloytth playnne cont[aining] iij helles quarter a nother cont[aining] ij helles quarter.

a cloytth of dyaper sore wornne cont[aining] iiij helles iij quarters.

TOWELLES OF DYAPER

Item viij* towelles on cont[aining] xiiij helles cont[aining] xij helles di cont[aining] ix helles cont[aining] x helles iij quarters xij helles quarter xv helles quartter v helles vij helles ij helles di v. helles quartter iiij helles di.

OTHER NESSYSARYS

Item ij grenne cloytthes of bavdekyn & on of blewe for weddynges.

a passion clotth to hange a ffore the Rudde a & whyte veylle to hange a ffore the hyghe avtter & a canabe of Red.

a cowsthen of Red veluet & ij deske cloytthes payntyd w^t ye passyon & ij lectornne cloytthes payntyd.

ij cowrtens of blew bokeram payntyd w^t angelles.

on† squarre cloytthes of damaske worke w^t ye crusyfyxe.

vj‡ syrplys & j§ myghters for sent nycolas & ij crysmatorys of sylke on of blewe and a nother yallow.

* xi erased and viii interlineated.
† ij erased and " on " interlineated.
‡ iij erased and vj interlineated.
§ Altered from " ij."

a sensser copper & gylt (w^t a schyppe)* & a ffyar panne & ij holly watter stockes of latton and xxxj boylles of latton ffor the Rudde loyft.

a payre of gret latton candelstyckes & ij peyres of candelstyckes of pryckes smalle & iij other peyrre of the myddyll sortte.

ij payrre of cruettes & ij pottes of pewtter w^t pypys.

(a blacke cloytth w a whytte crosse to ley on gravys.)*

iiij Rochettes for chyldern.

* Erased.

APPENDIX V

TESTAMENT AND WILL OF JOHN CROKE

Testament of John Croke.*

In dei nomine Amen Duodecimo die mensis Augusti Anno domini Millesimo cccc^{mo} septuagesimo septimo Ego Johannis Croke Ciuis et nuper Aldermannus Ciuitatis London' compos mentis ac sanus memorie laudetur altissimus existens condo facio et ordino presens testamentum meum in hunc qui sequitur modum In primis lego et recommendo animam meam misericordissimo Domino nostro Jhesu Cristo Creatori et saluatori meo beatissimeque Virgini matri eius gloriose et omnibus celi sanctis contra Inimicum humani generis defendendam Corpusque meum sepeliendum in ecclesia parochiali omnium sanctorum de Berkyng iuxta Turrim London' Item volo primo et principaliter quod tam cicius quam fieri poterit post meum decessum omnia debita que aliis de iure debeo fideliter persoluantur aut persolui prouideantur Et volo quod tunc omnia Residua bona mea et debita michi incumbencia per executores meos in tres partes equales diuidantur vnde lego Margarete vxori mee vnam partem nomine propartis sue omnium bonorum meorum mobilium et debitorum in sustentacionem eiusdem Margarete et exinde disponendam inxta suum libitum Secundam vero partem lego filiis meis videlicet Johanni Croke seniori Roberto Croke Thome Croke Ricardo Croke et Johanni Croke Juniori nomine proparcium eorundem de bonis meis mobilibus et debitis inter eos equaliter diuidendam disponendam et distribuendam per executores meos subscriptos Et volo quod predicta Margareta vxor mea sub sufficienti securitate pro ipsa in Camera Guihalde Ciuitatis London' secundum consuetudinem eiusdem Ciuitatis inuenienda habeat custodiam et gubernacionem omnium illorum bonorum que racione huius testamenti mei et presentis vltime voluntatis filius meis infra etatem existentibus pertinebunt videlicet donec et quousque huiusmodi filii mei sic infra etatem existentes ad plenam etatem viginti et vnius annorum peruenerint Et si aliquis seu aliqui eorundem filiorum meorum sic infra etatem existentes ante dictam etatem viginti et vnius annorum obierit vel obierint volo quod tunc vna medietas omnium bonorum cuiuslibet filiorum sic infra etatem decedentium remaneat domine Margarete Stokker filie mee vxori Willelmi Stokker militis Et quod altera medietas remaneat iiij^{o,} pueris videlicet Johanni Ryche filio Kateryne Johanne et Anne filiabus Elizabethe Stonor filie mee inter ipsam Elizabetham et Thomam Ryche defunctum nuper virum suum procreatis inter eosdem pueros equaliter diuidenda et participanda Et volo quod tercia pars omnium dictorum bonorum et debitorum meorum sic diuisorum et participatorum remaneat executoribus meis subscriptis adinde perimplendam voluntatem meam infraspecificatam Prouiso semper quod in dictis diuisione et participacione bonorum et debitorum meorum sorciatur et addatur cuilibet parti dictarum trium partum equalis et consimilis valor de omnibus iocalibus et vasis meis aureis et argenteis

* *P.C.C.*, 33 Wattys.

atque de vtensilibus et hustilimentis domicilio meo quouismodo spectantibus Item de dicta tertia parte omnium bonorum et debitorum meorum lego summo Altari dicte ecclesie omnium sanctorum pro oblacionibus meis oblitis aut negligenter detentis in anime mee exoneracionem et ad exorandum pro anima mea decem marcas Item lego operibus et edificacioni ecclesie predicte xl^{ta} libras exinde disponendas iuxta discrecionem executorum meorum Item lego ad disponendum in factura alte trabis videlicet de le Rodelofte eiusdem ecclesie et ad sustentacionem luminis eiusdem quadraginta libras Item lego pro vna secta vestimentorum emenda et ordinanda pro eadem ecclesia xl libras Item lego ad expendendum in libris pro eadem ecclesia emendis et ordinandis xl marcas Item lego fraternitate beate marie de Berkyng Chapell prope ecclesiam predictam xls. Item lego fraternitati corporis Cristi mistere pellipariorum london' Cs. Item lego fraternitati beate Marie pellipariorum london' xls. Item lego ad disponendum in Relauemen et sustentacionem prisonariorum in Newgate Ludgate et duobis Computatorijs London' et in prisonis de Marchalsey et Banco Regis in Southwerk existentium ac pauperum hominum et mulierum in hospitali de Bedlem london' et leprosorum hospitalium sancti Egidij Kyngeslond et le loke prope London' et aliorum domorum leprosorum infra sex miliaria Ciuitatem London' contigua et inter iiij^{or} ordines fratrum mendicancium London' ad exorandum pro salute anime mee et animarum parentum et benefactorum meorum C marcas inter eos diuidendas distribuendas et liberandas per discrecionem et ordinacionem executorum meorum. Item lego personis subscriptis summas subsequentes videlicet Johanni Croke seniori filio meo C li. Thome Buckley decem marcas Thome Corser quinque marcas Thome Morton xls. et Willelmo laurence xls. Emme Shetford xls. Johanne Moreton xxvjs. viijd. Thome Max duas marcas Thome Cooke xs. Ac filiis et filiabus Thome Riche x li. [Numerous other monetary bequests]. Item lego ad disponendum circa sepulturam meam et in exequiis meis debite exequendis centum marcas Residuum vero dicte tercie partis omnium bonorum per me dictis executoribus meis ad perficiendam meam vltimam voluntatem superius assignate et non supralegatum do et lego executoribus adinde disponendum in elemosinis et aliis piis vsibus prout eis melius videbitur pro salute anime mee fore facturis ac prout coram summo Judice inde respondere voluerint Huius autem testamenti mei et vltime voluntatis mee executores ordino et constituo videlicet predictam Margaretam vxorem meam dictum Willelmum Stokker militem Willelmum Essex Gentilman' et Robertum Tate Ac eorum superuisorem facio ordino et constituo Johannem Tate fratrem dicti Roberti Tate Et lego cuilibet executorum meorum onus execucionis dicti testamenti mei in se suscipienti pro suo labore xx marcas Et volo quod si forte contingat quod bona mea mobilia apud Calesiam et in partibus transmarinis existentia et debita mea ibidem michi debencia ad manus executorum meorum saluo et integre non denueniant quod absit Ita quod supradicta legata mea bene perimpleri nequeant quod tunc de omnibus legatis meis de tercia parte mea propria superius facta [*sic*] fiat equalis et consimilis defalcacio iuxta ratam et quantitatem cuiuslibet huiusmodi legati mei per discrecionem executorum

85

meorum subscriptorum   Item ego predictus Johannes Croke testator volo et lego per presentes quod dicta Margareta vxor mea vltra legatum suum predictum clare et libere habeat et teneat ad suum proprium vsum tam omnia vestimenta et ornamenta corpori suo spectantia quameciam omnia bona denarios et debita que ipsa Margareta ex lana mea habuit et inquisiuit racione proprie mercandisacionis sue.

[Proved at Lambeth 19 Nov. 1477 by the executors; a cross-reference is given in 15th-century hand to the last will of this John Croke, an abstract of which is as follows] :

[Last will* of John Croke, citizen and skinner and late Alderman of London, 26 Sept. 1477, touching all his lands and tenements within the city and suburbs of London, in the counties of Middlesex and Buckinghamshire and in the town of Calais.   To John Croke the elder my son all my tenements in Wode-strete and Siluerstrete and lands and tenements in Drayton [and elsewhere, co. Bucks].   To my wife Margaret for life all my lands & tenements in the city and suburbs of London, the county of Middlesex and the town of Calais.]   " Et volo quod prefata Margareta vxor mea de exitibus et proficuis predictarum terrarum et tenementorum cum eorum pertinenciis annuatim durante vita eiusdem Margarete a tempore mortis mee Inueniat et sustineat vnum capellanum idoneum diuina celebraturum in ecclesia Omnium sanctorum de Berking' London' ad altare sancti Nicholai in eadem ecclesia exorandum pro anima mea et animabus parentum amicorum et benefactorum meorum et omnium fidelium defunctorum Et volo etiam quod prefata Margareta vxor mea de exitibus et proficuis predictis annuatim durante vita sua teneri et obseruari faciat in predicta ecclesia omnium sanctorum eo tempore anni quo me prefatum Johannem Croke ab hac luce migrare contigerit pro anima mea et animabus predictis quendam obitum siue Anniversarium per notam per Vicarium capellanos et clericos eiusdem ecclesie videlicet cum placebo et dirige in vigilia et missa de Requiem in crastino sequenti ac cum pulsacione campanorum et aliis obseruanciis ob huiusmodi obitum congruis prout in tali casu in ciuitate London' fieri consuetum est Et quod dicta Margareta vxor mea disponat et distribuat annuatim durante vita sua ad predictum Anniversarium videlicet vicario capellanis et clericis eiusdem ecclesie ibidem interessentibus ac in aliis necessariis circa obitum predictum indigentibus et requisitis vjs. et viijd.' Et volo quod post decessum predicte Margarete vxoris mee totum illud mesuagium quod ego predictus Johannes Croke die date presencium inhabito situatum in venella vocata Martelane in parrochia omnium sanctorum de Berking' predicta cum gardino adiacenti et suis pertinentiis Acetiam duo tenementa eidem mesuagio annexata et adiacentia ex parte boriali eiusdem mesuagii situata in parrochia sancti Olaui prope toure-strete London' Necnon totum meum tenementum bracineum vocatum le Cuppe situatum prope wharuum vocatum le Newe Wolle keye in dicta par-

---

* *P.C.C.*, 4 Logge (Latin).

rochia omnium sanctorum de Berkyng' cedant et remaneant vicario ecclesie parochialis omnium sanctorum de Berking' predicte et Successoribus suis vicario euisdem ecclesie pro tempore existenti ac custodibus bonorum et ornamentorum eiusdem ecclesie et successoribus suis pro tempore existentibus Habenda et tenenda predictum mesuagium cum gardino adiacenti et suis pertinentiis ac dicta duo tenementa eidem messuagio annexata necnon totum tenementum bracineum vocatum le Cuppe cum omnibus suis pertinentiis prefatis vicario ac custodibus siue gardianis dicte ecclesie omnium sanctorum de Berkyng' et successoribus suis imperpetuum. . . . Ea intencione quod predictus vicarius et custodes siue gardiani et successores sui pro tempore existentes annuatim imperpetuum post mortem dicte Margarete vxoris mee de et cum exitibus et proficuis predicti mesuagii cum gardino . . . ac dictorum duorum tenementorum . . . necnon dicti tenementi bracinei . . . inueniant et sustineant unum capellanum idoneum diuina celebraturum in predicta ecclesia omnium sanctorum ad altare sancti Nicholai ibidem et ad orandum pro anima mea et animabus parentum meorum et omnium fidelium Defunctorum Et volo eciam quod prefati vicarius et custodes siue gardiani et successores sui post mortem predicte Margarete vxoris mee de et cum exitibus et proficuis predictis teneant et obseruent seu teneri et obseruari faciant annuatim imperpetuum in predicta ecclesia omnium sanctorum eo tempore anno quo me prefatum Johannem Croke ab hac luce migrare contigerit. . . . Anniversarium . . . prout supradictum est Expendendis et distribuendis annuatim circa huiusmodi. . . . Anniversarium xs . . . videlicet vicario capellanis et clericis eiusdem ecclesie et in ceteris necessariis circa huiusmodi obitum indigentibus et requisitis vjs. et viij d. Et quod de tribus solidis et iiij^or denariis residuis . . . vterque custodum dicte ecclesie capiat et habeat pro suo labore in premissis exequendis et ad superuidend' reparacionem ac sustentacionem terrarum et tenementorum xx denarios".

[Failing the observance of these conditions, the premises are to remain to the rector and wardens of St. Olave's to find a chaplain in that church under similar conditions].

[After the death of wife Margaret, the remaining tenements to remain as follows:

to my son John Croke the elder lands in Totenham and Edemeton co. Middx, the inn called le Royall in the parish of St. Thomas Ap. in Vintry Ward, and a tenement in Calais called ' le Shewhous '

To my son Robert Croke lands and tenements in Tourestrete London late acquired from Walter Vitull' armourer and John Hurst, skinner;

To my son Thomas Croke a tenement with brewhouse called le Swanne in Tourestrete with 2 tenements adjoining and my purparty of lands near Coldeharborowe, London, which I and Robert Tate late acquired of the executors of the lord de Vessey;

to my son Richard Croke lands and tenements in Westchepe in the parish of St. Giles and in Athelstrete;

87

to my son John Croke the younger 2 tenements in Fletestrete, a tenement in Aldrichgatestrete in Briggestrete, crofts in lyverlane and Bradfordebrigge near Holborn;

to my daughter Margaret wife of William Stokker knight my messuage or place in Chelchithe co. Middx].

'Presentibus ad declaracionem istius mee voluntatis Magistro Roberto Segrym vicario ecclesie parochialis omnium sanctorum de Berking' . . . et aliis'.

[Proved at Knolle 19 Nov. 1481 by the widow Margaret].

APPENDIX VI

TESTAMENT AND WILL OF ROBERT TATE*

[The Testament, 13 Nov. 1500]

' In the name of god amen The xiij^th day of the moneth of Nouembre [1500]. . . . I Robert Tate Alderman of the Citie of london and mercer of the same Citie . . . make . . . my present testament and last will in . . . forme ensuyng . . . my body to be buried in the chapell of our lady called Berking chapell beside the parisshe church of Alhalowen berkyng of London that is to wite, on the northside of the same chapell before thymage of o^r lady there, and as nygh to the wall as convenyently may be by the good discrecion of myne executors and ouerseers. . . . And I woll that myn executors herevndernamed of my goods doo to be made a fayr and sufficient arche in the said wall from Est to West w^t a chapell convenyent from the said arche toward the North as the ground ther woll gyve and reasonably may be sparyd, And that the same chapell be named and callid seynt Thomas chapell And in the Este ende therof A convenyent awter to be made for a preest to syng for my soule, and my wiffes our faders and moders frendes benefactors and all Christen soules, And w^t a table convenyent of seynt Thomas the martyr w^t his martyrdom therin conteyned to serve afore the high awter, and to be made by the avise and discrecion of myn executors. . . . And I woll that the costs and charges of my burying and funerall service shalbe doon in goode and honest maner . . . Also I woll that in all goodely haste after my burying all such dettes as I shall then owe . . . shalbe wele and truely . . . paid . . . in dischargying of my soule And than . . . all my goods . . . moevable . . . shalbe devided into iij eqall partes . . . all my stuff of household excepte plate . . . shalbe owte of the said particion And . . . I bequethe unto Margery my wife oon parte w^t all the seid stuff of household. . . . Another parte . . . vnto all my childern sones and daughters than lyving and not maryed evenly to be devided. . . . And the iij^d parte . . . I . . . assigne to be disposed for the helth of my soule and vnto my frendes in manner . . . ensuyng . . . to euery of my sones C li . . . to euery of my daughters C li. . . . Item. . . . I bequeth to the high awter of Berking church aforseid for myn offeryngs and dueties forgoten or necligently witholden in discharging of my soule, and to haue my soule praid fore x marcs . . . to the reparacion of the body of the forseid chapell of our lady beside Berkyng church, soo and vnder condicion that myn executors may be suffred to execute my will as in the Arche and Chapell makyng there for me as is aforeseid xx li . . . to be distributed in the prysons of london and nygh thereunto in brede at sundry tymes to pray for my soule. . . . In Newgate xls. In ludgate xls. In the Fleet xls. In the Marchalsey in Southwerk xxs. And in the kyngs benche xxs.'

[Bequests to four houses of Friars in London for ' Placebo and Dirige and masse of Regine. Immediatlye after my decesse', and to other friars,

* *P.C.C.*, 18 Moone.

H
89

priests and novices, in London to say Placebo and Dirige at leisure; to the Crutched Friars, Lazar Houses and the House of Syon, and the Charterhouse of Shene; toward the making of an altar cloth for the high altar in the Charterhouse beside London 'the which Dan William Bowre a brother of the same place is, worker thereof' 13s. 4d.; to the minoresses of London and Denny; other pious bequests for marriage of poor maidens of Coventry, repairs of Colsell and other churches including Coventry].

'Item I bequeth to the Mayre of London beyng atte tyme of my decesse soo that he be att my burying and moneths mynde as Mayre of the same Citie xxs. Item to the Recorder of the same Citie than and there beyng in lykewise vjs. viijd. Item I bequeth to the Chamberleyn common sergeant and common clerk of the same Citie attending vpon the Mayre at my said burying and moneths mynde bicause they be common officers of the said Citie I woll that euery of them thre shall haue for his labour vjs viijd. Item I will that euery Alderman and Shiriff of the said Citie being atte my seid burying and moneths mynd shall have for their labours that is to sey Euery Grey cloke xs. And euery Alderman of the Calabre cloke and Shiriff vjs. viijd. Item I bequeth to be distributed among the mynstralls called the waytes of London in consideracion of their grete labours and poure lyving x li sterling To be pute into the keping of the Chamberleyn of London. . . . And . . . distributed by hym amonges theym beyng from tyme to tyme in ten yeres next ensuyng after my decesse . . . for their better refresshing.'

[Numerous monetary bequests.]

'Item I bequeth C and lx li., therwith myn executors to bye . . . lands to the yerely value of viij li, or x li, . . . If in my liff tyme I doo it not myself, And wt the same lands and wt my tenements in More lane which I . . . bought of Bernes, I will that myn executors purvey and doo establisshe A preest perpetually to syng in the said chapell which I haue afore . . . assigned to be made oute of the said chapell called or lady chapell on the Northside of the same, lyke as hereafter in the will of my lands more playnly it is declared Prouided allway that if it happen any of my goods by casueltie or malefortune to be loste wherby ther shall lak of my said iijd parte to fulfill this my last will . . . it shalbe borne of all the iij parts of my goods'. . . .

[*The will, made on same date*]: . . . First I will that myn executours . . . wth the Clxli by me . . . assigned . . . in all goodely haste after my decesse shall purchace . . . goode land to the yerely value of viij li. or xli. . . . And of the seid lands . . . and of my tenement in Morlane which I late bought of Barnes I woll that the shall doo establissh and amortise . . . A chauntry after the manner and custome of the Citie of London of oon preest, an honest man and well disposed perpetually to synge for my soule and other the soules in my testament aforerehersed in the chapell which

90

bifore in my said testament I have appoynted to be made w^t an Arche on the Northside of o^r lady Berkyng chapell. The same preest to haue yerely for his salary vij li. And also I woll that myn executours in thestablisshment . . . of the said Chauntry doo provide . . . that myn obite be kept in the said chapell called Berkynge chapell yerely for euermore, about suche tyme and season of the yere as it shall happen me to departe this life. . . . Expending . . . yerely for . . . the same obit xs. And xxs. yerely of the revenue . . . shall goo toward the mayntenance of o^r lady masse and Anteyn by note within the same chapell called Berkyng chapell And vjd wekely . . . to an honest poure man to attende in the said chapell, and to helpe the seid preest to syng, And if eny thing remayne . . . it shall goo . . . to the comen box of the said chapell by the Master and Wardeyns of the same chapell . . . to be disposed . . . in defense repayring and mayntenance of the same lyvelode . . . the settyng in and presentacion of the said preest the ouersight of the seide obite and lyvelode and the payments aforseide shalbe assigned . . . to the maister and Wardeyns of our lady chapell and to their successors. And if they defawte . . . the said londes and tenements shall remayn to the Chamberleyn of London . . . fynding and doyng w^t the same lykewise. . . .

[Lands in London, Coventry, Essex, Kent, Hertfordshire, Berkshire and Warwickshire to be divided into two, ' Excepte alwey oute of the same particion my grete Mes' wherein I dwell sett in the parisshe of Alhalowen Berkyng beside the tour of London, and also my tenement in Morelane ' . . . [one part to wife Margery " w^t my seid grete Mes' wherein I dwell," the other to my eldest son Robert Tate.]

[Appoints wife Margery, brother John Tate and Thomas Marrow executors.]

Proved by Margaret [*sic*] Tate the widow 26 Jan. 1500/01.

BIBLIOGRAPHICAL NOTE

Collections in illustration of the Parochial History and Antiquities of the Ancient Parish of All Hallows Barking, in the City of London, by Joseph Maskell, Curate of All Hallows Barking, 1864. A copy with the Author's MSS. and notes added 1868–9 is at the British Museum. Press-mark 10358.i.5.

All Hallows Barking Church, London: A brief History of the Ancient Church and Parish, by Rev. Joseph Maskell, Master of Emanuel College, Westminster, and late Curate of All Hallows. (A pamphlet.) Undated. *c.* 1885.

Transactions of S. Paul's Ecclesiological Society. " Sᵗ· Olave's, Hart St., and All Hallows Barking " (with plans), by Philip Norman, F.S.A., LL.D.

London Topographical Society's Record, Vol. V, p. 108. " London City Churches that escaped the Great Fire," by Philip Norman, F.S.A., LL.D.

Transactions of the London and Middlesex Archæological Society, Vol. II, 1863, p. 125 *et seq.* " Vicars of All Hallows," by Joseph Maskell.

Transactions of the London and Middlesex Archæological Society, N.S. Vol. V, 1923. " Richard Cœur de Lion and the Church of All Hallows Barking," by Philip Norman, F.S.A., LL.D.

All Hallows Barking : The Story and Work of " Berkyngechurche " by the Tower, by C. R. Davey Biggs, D.D., 1912.

All Hallows Barking and the Memorial to William Penn. The Pennsylvania Society, New York, 1911.

" Berkyngechirche " (a pamphlet). Reprint of an article by Canon A. J. Mason, published 1927.

In addition to references in all the principal Histories of London, such as those by Stow, Strype, Maitland, Wheatley and Cunningham, Wilkinson, Hughson, mention may be made of the accounts in—

Benham's *Old London Churches*, pp. 35–43, with an interior view.

Jenkinson's *London Churches*, pp. 83–88.

Malcolm's *Londinium Redivivum*, Vol. II, pp. 415–25.

Clarke's *City Churches*.

Godwin and Britton's *Churches of London*, Vol. I.

Daniell's *London City Churches*, pp. 14–27.

Ellwood (G. M.) and Day (E. H.). *Some London Churches*, 1911, pp. 1–4

Bumpus (T. F.). *Churches, Ancient and Modern*, Vol. I, pp. 164–66.

Gentleman's Magazine. 1815, Pt. 1, pp. 35, 36; 1928, Pt. 1, p. 582 1844, Pt. 2, pp. 484–86.

Notes and Queries. December 6, 1890.

A Sepia Wash Drawing, 1813. Now in the Bishopsgate Institute. L. 34, Vol. I.

INDEX TO NAMES

Page

Abbott, Edward, A. M. – – 42, 53
Abbott, George, Archbishop of Canterbury – – – – – 42
Acre, fall of – – – – – 6
Agas – – – – – – 55
Aldermen of London, see London
Aldersgate Street – – – – 88
Aleyn, Sir John – – – – 18
All Hallows the Great, Church of – – 3
All Souls' College, Oxford – – 10
Amuresden, Richard – – – 10, 28
Andrewes, Lancelot, Bishop of Winchester 39
Andrews, Alderman – – – 44
Andrews, Captain Eusebius – – 43
Antwerp – – – – – 55
Archbishops of Canterbury, see Canterbury
Archer, Widow – – – – 20
Arley, John – – – – 18
Armar, William – – – – 39
Aschewell, William – – – 78
Aswey (or Eswy), Stephen, Alderman – 5
Athelstrete (Addle Street) – – 87
Attemille, Thomas – – – 24, 71
Audit House – – – – 47
Augmentations, Court of – – 3
Austin, David – – – – 48
Awgoure, Nicholas – – – 38
Awood, James – – – – 19
Aylesford, Kent – – – – 41
Aylmer, Bishop of London – – 38

Bacheler, Walter le – – – 7
Bacheworth, Margaret de – – 8
Baker, John – – – – 30
Baldry, Richard, A. M. – – 52
Barker, John – – – – 16
Barkin, Thomas – – – – 40
Barking, Abbess of – – – 1, 2
Barking, Abbey of – – 1, 2, 3, 9
Barking Alley – – – – 56
Barnes, otherwise Bernes – – 90
Barnes, Dr. Robert – – 35, 37
Barons of the Exchequer – – 8
Bath and Wells, Ken, Thomas, Bishop of 51
Batman, John – – – – 36
Beamontie, Hipolitan – – – 19
Beamontie, otherwise Bennye, Thomas – 19
Beare Yarde – – – – 40
Beaufort, Cardinal – – – 17
Beaven – – – – – 67
Bedlam, Hospital of – – – 85
Beer Lane – – – – 45, 46
Benalius, Hieronimus – – – 39
Bene, Nicholas – – – – 30

Page

Bennye, otherwise Beamontie, Thomas – 19
Bergamo – – – – – 39
Berkshire – – – – – 91
Bermondsey, Prior of – – – 8
Bethel, Slingsby, M.P., Lord Mayor – 65
Betson, Thomas – – – – 24
Billingsgate – – – – 12, 67
Bishops, see under Name of See and of Individual
Blackwell, Master – – – 47
Blakelofte, a tenement in Mark Lane – 32
Blakeney, Adam – – – 32, 33
     Cecily, wife of Peter – – 32
     Peter – – – – 9, 31, 32
Bland, Faith – – – – 40
"Blewebolle," a ship – – – 9
Bolle, John – – – – 28
Bonner, Bishop of London – – 3
Boroughbridge, Battle of – – 8
Bourchier, Sir Robert, Chancellor – 8, 9
Bow Lane – – – – 19
Bowre, Dan William – – – 90
Boy Bishop – – – 26, 31
Bradfordebrigge – – – – 88
Brathwell, Mr. – – – – 47
Braybroke, Bishop of London – 33
Brayton, Thomas de – – – 9
Breton, Thomas – – – – 30
Brewers' Company – – – 66
Brichtwen, Wife of Riculf – – 1
Bridge Street – – – – 88
Bristol—
     Canynges of – – – 13
     Mouton, Nicholas, of – – 6
Broad Street – – – – 19
Broke, Thomas de – – – 2, 52
Bryan, Katherine – – – – 40
Bryan, Thurlow or Tirlowe – – 40
Brymmesgrove, Sir Nicholas, or Bromesgrove (Vicar) – – 23, 33, 52, 74
Buckinghamshire – – – – 86
     Drayton – – – – 86
Buckley, Thomas – – – – 85
Bulbecke, Alexander de – – 6
Burdon, Major Richard – – 50
Burgyn, Geoffrey – – – 33
Burnell, John – – – – 41

Caas, Thomas – – – – 52
Calais – – – 27, 29, 85, 86, 87
Calais, Merchants of Staple of 16, 24, 35
Calamy, Edmund – – – 47
Cambridge – – – – 49
Cambridge, Alice, Wife of John (I) of – 32

	Page
Cambridge, John (I) of – – –	32, 33
John (II) of – – – – –	32
Canterbury – – – – –	68
Archbishop of – – – – –	3, 51
Abbot, George – – – –	42
Chichele, Henry – – – –	10
Grindall – – – – –	3
Kempe, John – – – –	17
Laud, William – – 42, 43, 44, 51
Whitgift, John – – – –	39
Canterbury, Christchurch (i.e. the Cathedral), Prior and Chapter of – –	68
Canynges, Thomas – – – –	13
Cardinal Beaufort – – – –	17
Carter, J. – – – – –	55, 56
Carter, Robert, S.T.B. – – – –	52
Castelyn, James – – – –	19
Caterton, Robert – – – –	70
Cecily, Duchess of York – – –	14
Cestreton, William de – – –	6
Chaluz – – – – –	12
Chamberlain of London – – –	90
Chancellors—	
Bourchier, Sir Robert – –	8
Robert, Bishop of Chichester –	8
Lord, Jeffreys, George – –	49
of the Exchequer, Master John Somerset – – –	13, 14
Chancery, Court of – – –	2, 8
Chappell Alley – – – –	20
Charles I, King – – – –	44
Charles II, King – – –	48, 49
Charterhouse—	
London – – – – –	90
Shene – – – – –	90
Chatterton, Edmund – – –	52
Chaucer, Geoffrey – – –	37
Chelsea – – – – –	88
Chester, Robert – – – –	82
Chichele, Henry, Archbishop of Canterbury – – – – –	10
Robert, Sir – – – –	10
Thomas – – – –	10
Chichele's Rents in Tower Street –	10, 18
Chichester, Bishop of – – –	7
Robert, Bishop of – –	8
Chicken Lane – – –	6, 10, 20
Chigwell, Hamon de – – –	8
Chilworth, Henry Polsted of –	18
Chitterling Alley – – –	45, 46
Chitty, Sir Thomas, Lord Mayor –	65
Cholmondeley, Sir Richard, Kt. –	17
Christ's Hospital – – –	40, 60
Churche, John – – – –	23
Churches of London, see under respective dedications	
Clarence, Duke of – – –	14
Clayton, Philip Thomas Byard –	53

	Page
Clements, Mr. (Churchwarden) – –	49
Clendon, Thomas – – 43, 47, 48
Clerke, John – – – –	52
Clif, Master William – – –	13
Cockayne, George – – –	43
Cok, John – – – – 10, 30, 54
Coke, Lawrence – – – –	30
Coldharbour, London – – –	87
Colles, William – – – –	52
Colleton, Ann – – – –	61
Colsell (? Coleshill, Co. Warwickshire) –	90
Colt, Thomas – – – –	14
Colyn, John – – –	29, 31
Richard – – – 28, 29, 30, 31
Rose – – –	29, 31
Common Clerk of London – –	90
Common Sergeant of London –	90
Compayne, Bartholomew – –	19
Compters (Prisons) – – –	85
Cooke, Thomas – – –	85
Cornhill, Tun prison on – –	4
Corser, Thomas – – –	85
Coton, Robert – – –	52
Cotton, George – – –	19, 36
Covell, Francis – – –	42, 44
Margaret or Margery –	42, 63
Coventry – – –	90, 91
Church of St. Michael at –	17, 90
Crabbe, Nicholas – – –	5
Crathorne, Thomas – –	42, 63
Crawley, Co. Oxon – – –	4
Croke, John (Alderman) 14, 21, 27, 30, 31, 32, 33, 34, 36, 75, 84, 85, 86, 87, 88
John, eldest son of above – 84, 85, 86, 87
John, Junior, youngest son of above 84, 88
Margaret, widow, of – 32, 84, 85, 86, 87, 88
Richard – – – –	84, 87
Robert – – – –	84, 87
Thomas – – –	84, 87
Crome, Dr. (Edward) – –	35, 37
Cromwell, Thomas – – –	35
Crosley, George – – –	50
Croucheman, John – – –	6
Crutched Friars, house of –	2, 90
Cup Brewhouse – – –	86, 87
Curfew – – – –	4
Customs, Farmers of – –	42
Dalby, Thomas de – –	52
Danes – – – –	1
Daniel (Curate) – – –	37
Danyell, John – – –	37
Darynoun, Jacominus – –	8
Davyers, Richard – – –	18
Dawes, William, LL.B. – 36, 37, 38, 52
Deacon, William – – –	45
Dekins, Elizabeth – – –	49
Denham or Dennam, William – 36, 78

94

	Page
Denny, Abbess of — — — — —	35
Minoresses of — — — — —	90
Dennys, Philip — — — — —	37
Deptford — — — — — —	12
Derlove, Ralph — — — — —	52
Dobbes, John — — — — —	30
Dolphin Tavern — — — — —	48
Drapers' Company — — — —	66
Drayton, Co. Bucks — — — —	86
Drewe, Richard — — — — —	18
Duddyngton, Anthony — — — —	25
Dudley, John, Earl of Warwick — —	18
Durham — — — — — —	62
Dyrham, Co. Gloucestershire — —	19
Dyxe, John — — — — — —	77
Eastcheap — — — — — —	29, 45
Edmonton — — — — —	69, 87
Edward I, King — 5, 11, 12, 13, 16, 67, 68
II, — — — — 6, 7, 8, 9
III, — — — 2, 8, 9, 14, 32
IV, — — 3, 9, 14, 15, 16, 18
VI, — — 19, 31, 36, 37, 39, 44
Edward, the Black Prince — — —	23
Edwards of London (Coat of Arms) —	66
Elizabeth, Queen — 19, 37, 39, 40, 44
Ely House — — — — — —	43
Isle of — — — — — 11, 12, 67
Enfield — — — — — —	50
Ereth, John — — — — —	70
Erkenwald, St., Bishop of London — —	1
Essex (County) — — — — —	91
Moulsham — — — — —	36
Radminster — — — — —	48
Rivenhall — — — — —	36
Tollesbury — — — — —	2
Woodham Walter — — — —	36
Essex, William — — — — —	85
Evers, Robert — — — — —	20
Evesham, Thomas de — — — —	9
Evinger or Evyngar, Ellen — — —	18
Evinger or Evyngar, John — — 18, 30
Exchequer — — — — — —	37
Barons of — — — — —	8
Chancellor of, Master John Somerset 13, 14
Eyles, Sir John, Bart., Lord Mayor —	65
Faithorne — — — — — —	55
Fauconer, Richard — — — 25, 29
Robert — — — — —	25
Fetter Lane — — — — —	9
Fillett, Goody Mary — — — —	46
Fishe, John — — — — — —	66
Fisher, John, Bishop of Rochester — —	34
Fishmongers' Company — — —	65
Fleet Prison — — — — —	89
Fleet Street — — — — —	88
Ford, Sir Richard — — — —	48
Forster, Edmund — — — 42, 63

	Page
Foucher, John — — — — —	52
Foyle, James — — — — —	50
Framlingham — — — — —	35
Friars Mendicants — — — —	85
Frowick, Henry — — — — —	13
Fuller, Hugh — — — — —	3
Fuller, Mr., "the Wit of Cambridge" —	49
Fyssher, John — — — — —	30
Fyssher, Mr. — — — — —	38
Galleymen — — 22, 23, 24, 30, 72, 75
Galley Quay — — — — —	30
Garret, Thomas — — — —	38
Gascoyne — — — — —	55
Gaskarth, John, A. M. — — —	53
Gattewicke, William de — — —	52
Gedding or Gedyng, William — 52, 78
Geekle, William — — — —	53
Gennyns or Janing, Nicholas — 29, 78
Gibbons, Grinling — — — —	50
Gilbert, Bishop of London — — 11, 13, 68
Gilbert, Thomas — — — 30, 35
Giles, William — — — — —	41
Glamuile, Richard de — — —	9
Gloucester, Humphrey, Duke of — —	17
Richard, Duke of — — —	14
Thomas Ravis, Bishop of — —	39
Gloucestershire, Dyrham — — —	19
Goddard, Elizabeth — — — —	4
Godfrey, John — — — — —	4
Godyng, William — — — —	33
Goodwin, Mr. (the Mathematician)
42, 55, 57, 58
Grapenel or Grapynell, Walter — 9, 52
Great Tower Street — — — —	54
Greenwich — — — — —	35
Gremet, John — — — — — 6, 9
Grey, Thomas, Lord — — —	37
Grimwade, Mr. — — — — —	42
Grindall, Archbishop of Canterbury —	3
Grobbe, Edward — — — —	9
Gryffen, Rychard — — — —	78
Grymesby, Sir Edmund de — — —	9
Guildhall — — — — — —	84
Haberdashers' Company — — —	65
Hague, The — — — — —	48
Hall, Dr. Joseph — — — —	44
Hancockes, John — — — —	36
Harlyston, John — — — —	52
Harmon, Richard — — — —	40
Harris, Renatus — — — 49, 62
Harrison and Harrison — — —	62
Hawkes, Sir William — — —	27
Haydok, Dame Margery — 22, 23, 24, 74
Haynnes, John — — — — —	19
Hayward — — — — — —	55
Hebson, Agnes — — — — —	46

Page

Henham, Margaret – – – – 29
Henry II, King – – – – – 1
  III, – – – – 11, 14, 67
  IV, – – – – 2, 10, 14
  VI, – – 13, 14, 15, 16, 70
  VII, – – – – 3, 16
  VIII, 3, 16, 25, 27, 34, 35, 36, 39, 78
Hertfordshire – – – – – 91
Heth, William – – – – – 10
Hewett, Goodwife – – – – 41
Hewett, Roger – – – – – 28
Hickes or Hicks, Dr. George, S.T.P. 50, 53
Higham Ferrers, Northamptonshire – 10
Hobbes, John – – – – – 70
Holborn – – – – – – 88
Hollar – – – – – – 55
Holy Trinity, Priory of, London – 6, 26
Hotham, John, Esq. – – – – 43
  Sir John – – – – – 43
Howell, Mrs. – – – – – 50
Hugh, Simon or Symkyn – 10, 27, 30, 75
Hughes, Geoffrey – – – – 23
Hull – – – – – – 43
Humphrey, Duke of Gloucester – – 17
Hurar, Isabel – – – – – 36
Hurer, Geoffrey le – – – – 9
Hurst, John – – – – – 87
Hykedy, Robert – – – – – 32

Iford, John – – – – – 52
Ingo, Robert – – – – – 27
Innocent VI, Pope – – – – 2
Italy – – – – – – 30

James, Roger – – – – – 39
James I, King – – – – – 44
Janing, Nicholas – – – – 52
Jeffreys, George, Judge, Lord Chancellor 49
Jend . . ., George – – – – 66
Jenninge, Maurice de – – – – 52
Jenyn or Gennyns, Nicholas – – 29, 78
Jews – – – – – 12, 67
Jezard, Eleanor – – – – 46
  Jacob – – – – – 46
" John "—a lighter – – – – 10
John II, King of France – – 10, 23
John the Waterbearer – – – 5
Johnes, Sir Samuel – – – – 53
Johnson, Aleyn – – – 3, 30
Johnson, Elizabeth – – – 3, 30
Juda, wife of Marlibrun – – 12, 67

Kagrer, Laurence de – – – – 52
Kempe, John, Archbishop of Canterbury 17
Ken, Thomas, Bishop of Bath and Wells 51
Kent – – – – – – 91
  Aylesford – – – – – 41
Kervyle, John – – – – 16, 27

Page

Kettlewell, John – – – – – 50
Kildesby, William de – – – – 8
King's Bench Prison – – – 85, 89
Kingsland, Leper Hospital of St. Giles at– 85
Kirfote or Kyrfote, William – – 17, 36
Knight, William – – – – 46
Knights Templars – – – – 6
Knolle – – – – – 88
Knollys, Sir Robert – 23, 24, 33, 71, 75

Laine, Mr. – – – – – 42
Lambert, Charles Edmund – – – 53
Lambeth – – – – – 86
Lancaster, Earl of – – – – 8
Lane, Mark – – – – – 40
Latimer, Hugh, Bishop of Worcester 35, 37
Laud, William, Archbishop of Canterbury
                          42, 43, 44, 51
Laurence, William – – – – 85
Layfield, Dr. Edward 42, 43, 44, 48, 49, 53, 56
Lazar Houses of London – – – 90
Lee, George – – – – – 47
Lock Hospital – – – – – 85
Lollards – – – – – 12
London—
  Aldermen of – – – 5, 66, 90
    Andrews – – – – 44
    Aswey or Eswy, Stephen – – 5
    Croke, John – 14, 21, 27, 30, 31,
                      32, 33, 34, 36, 75,
                      84, 85, 86, 87, 88
    Monmouth, Humphrey – 35, 37
    Olney, John – – – 13
    Tate, Sir Robert, see list of Lord Mayors
  Bishops of – – 7, 20, 32, 35, 42, 48
    Aylmer – – – – 38
    Bonner – – – – 3
    Braybroke – – – – 33
    Erkenwald, St. – – – 1
    Gilbert – – – 11, 13, 68
    Ravis, Thomas – – – 39
  Bridge – – – – 37, 48
  Chamberlain of – – – – 90
  Charterhouse of – – – – 90
  Common Clerk of – – – 90
  Common Sergeant of – – – 90
  Companies of—
    Brewers – – – – 66
    Drapers – – – – 66
    Fishmongers – – – – 65
    Haberdashers – – – 65
    Salters – – – – 65
    Skinners – – – 29, 45
  County Council – – – – 55
  Lazar Houses of – – – 85, 90
  Lord Mayor, Court of – – – 48
  Mayors and Lord Mayors of – 5, 47, 90
    Bethel, Slingsby, M.P. – – 65

96

London—
  Mayors and Lord Mayors of—(contd.)—
    Canynges, Thomas   —   —   —   13
    Chichele, Sir Robert   —   —   —   10
    Chigwell, Hamon de   —   —   —   8
    Chitty, Sir Thomas   —   —   —   65
    Eyles, Sir John, Bart. —   —   —   65
    Rokesley, Gregory de   —   —   —   5
    Starling or Sterlinge, Sir Samuel — 66
    Tate, Sir Robert 11, 16, 17, 18, 20, 25,
                          85, 87, 89, 90, 91
    Whittington, Richard   —   —   —   10
  Minoresses of   —   —   —   —   —   90
  Prisons of   —   —   —   —   43, 89
    Compters   —   —   —   —   —   85
    Ely House   —   —   —   —   —   43
    Fleet   —   —   —   —   —   89
    Galleys on Thames   —   —   —   —   43
    King's Bench   —   —   —   —   85, 89
    Ludgate   —   —   —   —   85, 89
    Marshalsea   —   —   —   —   85, 89
    Newgate   —   —   —   —   85, 89
    Tun, Cornhill —   —   —   —   —   4
  Recorder of   —   —   —   —   —   90
  Sheriffs of   —   —   —   —   — 5, 90
  Streets, etc., of—
    Aldersgate Street —   —   —   —   88
    Athelstrete (Addle Street)   —   —   87
    Barking Alley —   —   —   —   —   56
    Beare Yarde   —   —   —   —   —   40
    Beer Lane   —   —   —   —   45, 46
    Billingsgate   —   —   —   —   12, 67
    Bow Lane   —   —   —   —   —   17
    Bridge Street —   —   —   —   —   88
    Broad Street   —   —   —   —   —   19
    Chappel Alley —   —   —   —   —   20
    Chichele's Rents, Tower Street   10, 18
    Chicken Lane   —   —   —   6, 10, 20
    Chitterling Alley —   —   —   45, 46
    Cornhill   —   —   —   —   —   4
    Eastcheap   —   —   —   —   —   29
    Fetter Lane   —   —   —   —   —   9
    Fleet Street   —   —   —   —   —   88
    Great Tower Street —   —   —   —   54
    Holborn   —   —   —   —   —   88
    Lyver Lane (now Leather Lane)   —   88
    Mark Lane   —   —   9, 32, 33, 36, 86
    Mincing Lane   —   —   —   —   —   30
    More (Moor) Lane —   —   —   90, 91
    Pety Wales   —   —   — 10, 28, 29, 30
    Priest's Alley —   —   —   45, 46, 47
    Queenhithe   —   —   —   —   —   17
    Roomland   —   —   —   —   —   20
    St. Katherine's Rents —   —   —   —   40
    Seething Lane 18, 19, 20, 23, 36, 48, 49
    Silver Street —   —   —   —   —   86
    Smithfield   —   —   —   —   —   37
    Spurier (now Water) Lane   —   —   33

London—
  Streets, etc., of—(contd.)—
    Tower Hill – 13, 15, 34, 35, 37, 43, 44
    Tower Street   —   —   16, 18, 40, 44,
                            45, 47, 48, 87
    Trinity Square —   —   —   —   20, 51
    Water (formerly Spurier) Lane   —   33
    Westchepe   —   —   —   —   —   87
    Wood Street   —   —   —   —   —   86
  Tower of   —   —   2, 4, 7, 12, 35, 43
    Chapel of St. Peter ad Vincula within 2, 14
    Constable of, Tiptoft, Earl of
        Worcester —   —   —   —   14
    Governors of—
        Churche, John —   —   —   —   23
        Hughes, Geoffrey   —   —   —   23
    Master Gunner of, Fauconer,
        Richard   —   —   25, 30
    Postern of –   —   —   —   —   —   6
    Watergate of   —   —   —   —   —   35
  Waits of   —   —   —   —   —   90
Lord Chancellor, Jeffreys, George –   —   49
Loseley Park, Surrey —   —   —   —   18
Lovell, John   —   —   —   —   —   31
Ludgate Prison   —   —   —   —   85, 89
Lyver (now Leather) Lane   —   —   —   88

Machen, John   —   —   —   —   —   52
Mark Lane   —   —   9, 32, 33, 36, 86
Marlibrun   —   —   —   —   12, 67
Marprelate Tracts —   —   —   —   —   39
Marrow, Thomas   —   —   —   —   —   91
Marshalsea Prison —   —   —   —   85, 89
Mary I, Queen   —   —   —   — 19, 37, 39
Mary II, Queen and William III –   —   50
Maskell, Revd. Joseph —   —   —   55, 62
Mason, Arthur James, D.D., Canon   53, 56
Mason, John   —   —   —   —   —   70
Max, Thomas   —   —   —   —   —   85
Mayssey, Robert   —   —   —   —   —   78
Medford or Metforde, Blanche   —   28, 76
Medford, Master   —   —   —   —   —   77
Merston, John   —   —   —   —   —   13
Michell, Nicholas —   —   —   —   18, 36
Middlesex   —   —   —   — 27, 86, 88
    Chelsea   —   —   —   —   —   88
    Edmonton   —   —   —   —   69, 87
    Enfield   —   —   —   —   —   50
    Tottenham   —   —   —   —   —   87
Mildmay, Thomas   —   —   —   —   —   36
Mincing Lane   —   —   —   —   —   30
Minoresses of Denny —   —   —   —   90
    of London   —   —   —   —   —   90
Monmouth, Humphrey, Alderman   35, 37
Morbek, Denys de   —   —   —   —   —   10
More Lane (now Moor Lane) —   90, 91
More, Sir Thomas   —   —   —   —   —   34
More, William, of Loseley Park, Surrey 18

	Page
More, William de la — — — —	6
Morena — — — — — —	49
Moreton, John (or Joan) — — —	85
Morris, William — — — — —	20
Mortilman, Joan — — —	28, 30
Morton, Thomas — — — —	85
Motoun, Nicholas — — — —	6
Moulsham, Co. Essex — — — —	36
Mulvard, Cecily le — — — —	28
Navy Office — — — —	49, 50
Naylor, John — — — — —	52
Neale, Robert — — — — —	44
Neesham, Sarah — — — — —	49
Newcourt — — — — — —	68
Newgate Prison — — — —	85, 89
Nicholas—Parish Priest — — —	33
Non-Jurors — — — — —	50
Norham — — — — —	12, 68
Northamptonshire, Higham Ferrers —	10
Northflete, Master Thomas, Canon of	
St. Paul's — — — — —	20
Northumberland, Norham — —	12, 68
Northwold, William — — — —	52
Oates, Titus — — — — —	50
Old Bailey — — — — — —	50
Olney, John, Alderman — — —	13
Oxford — — — — — —	37
Oxford, All Souls' College — —	10
St. John's College — —	43
Oxfordshire, Crawley — — —	4
Witney — — — — —	4
Pakyn, John — — — — —	27
Paling, John — — — — —	5
Papworth — — — — — —	66
Parish, Charles — — — — —	40
Pattenson, William — — — —	52
Payn, William — — — —	70, 74
Pearson, F. L. — — — — —	56
Peckham, Henry — — — —	37
Penn, Admiral Sir William — —	49
Penn, William — — — — —	49
Pennsylvania — — — — —	49
Pepys, Samuel — — —	49, 50, 59
Perkins, William — — — —	44
Pety Wales — — 10, 28, 29, 30
Philip II of Spain — — — —	37
Philippa, Queen — — — —	6
Phillip, King of France — — —	6
Phillips—Curate — — — —	38
Pilkes, Thomas — 9, 11, 31, 33, 36
Pitts, Widow — — — — —	46
Poitiers, Battle of — — —	10, 23
Polsted, Henry, of Chilworth —	18
Pontrell, John — — —	21, 75
Pope Innocent VI — — — —	2

	Page
Poperinghe — — — — —	51
Porter, Robert — — — —	45
Samuel — — — — —	45
Pownsett, William — — — —	3
Pownson, John — — — —	29
Price, G. — — — — —	66
Priest's Alley — — — 45, 46, 47
Prise, Robert — — — —	46
Quays, Wharves, etc.—	
Galley Quay — — — —	30
New Wool Quay — — —	86
Queenhithe — — — —	17
Wool Wharf — — — —	5
Queenhithe — — — —	17
Radminster, Co. Essex — —	48
Railway, Underground — —	20
Ram's Head in Eastcheap — —	29
Ravis, Thomas, S.T.B., Bishop of	
Gloucester and London —	39, 52
Recorder of London — — —	90
Reve, Thomas — — —	19, 36
Rich, Richard — — — —	13
Richard, Duke of Gloucester —	14
Duke of York — —	14
I, King, Cœur de Lion	
9, 11, 12, 13, 67, 68
II, — — — 2, 23, 32
III, — — — 3, 14, 16
Richardson, John — —	50
Richardson, Mr., Parish Clerk —	34
Riculf — — — — 1, 54
Rivenhall, Co. Essex — —	36
Robert, Bishop of Chichester —	8
Robert, George — — —	46
Robinson, Arthur William — —	53
Rochester, Cathedral of — —	1
Monks of — — 1, 54
Fisher, John, Bishop of — —	34
Walter, Bishop of — —	1
Rokesley, Gregory de, Mayor —	5
Rolff, John — — 10, 28, 30
Roomland — — — —	20
Rose Tavern — — 45, 46, 55
Rouen — — — —	12
Royal Inn — — — —	87
Rudde, John — — — —	36
Rutland, Earl of — — —	14
Ryche, Anne — — — —	84
Elizabeth — — —	84
Joan — — — —	84
John — — — —	84
Katherine — — —	84
or Riche, Thomas — —	84, 85
Rysley, Sir John — — 16, 17, 18, 19
St. Andrew by the Wardrobe, Church of	45

	Page
St. Andrew Undershaft, Church of	59
St. Armagilus, Image of	4
St. Christopher, Stocks, Parish of	19
St. Clement, Eastcheap, Church of	45
St. Dunstan in the East, Parish of	40
St. Erkenwald, Bishop of London	1
St. Giles' Parish	87
St. Gregory, Church of	47
St. John of Jerusalem, Prior of	8
St. John's College, Oxford	43
St. Katherine Cree, Church of	65
St. Katherine's Rents	40
St. Lawrence, Jewry, Church of	4
St. Magnus, John de	52
St. Margaret, Lothbury, Church of	2
St. Martin's le Grand	4
St. Mary Graces, Abbey of	32
St. Michael, Church of, at Coventry	17
St. Olave, Hart Street, Church of	20, 32, 49, 50, 86, 87
St. Paul's Cathedral	7, 20, 21, 43, 69
Cross	35
St. Peter ad Vincula within the Tower, Chapel of	2, 10, 14
St. Thomas Apostle, Parish of	87
Salarse, Sir Thomas	17
Salters' Company	65
Salueyn or Salveyn, Sibyl	10, 30
Sargonsces, Edmond	78
Sarum, use of	21
Saunders, Jonathan	49
Scot, Sir John, Kt.	14
Scotland	12, 44
Scots	68
Scott, John	25
Seething Lane	18, 19, 20, 23, 36, 48, 49
Segrym, Robert	52, 88
Shaw, Hester	47
Shene, Charterhouse of	90
Shepherd, Benjamin	44
Sheriffs of London	90
Sherington, Walter	69
Sherman, Edmund	50
Shetford, Emme	85
"Shewhouse"—a tenement	87
Shute, Walter	42
Silver Street	86
Skinners' Company	29, 45
Sluys, Battle of	8
Smithfield	37
Smyth (Vestryman)	40
Smythe, Grace	19
Richard	19
Robert	19
Snayth, George	43
Snetesham, Joan	30
Thomas	30
Somerset, Master John, Chancellor of the Exchequer	13, 14
"Sopehouse"—a tenement	36
Southhouse—coat of arms	66
Southwark	85, 89
Spicer, Dennis	17
Spurier (now Water) Lane	33
"Stapledehall"—a tenement	2
Starling or Sterlinge, Sir Samuel, Lord Mayor	66
Stephen, King	1
Stephen, Sir—a chaplain	33
Stephens, Jane	46
Steple	68
Stinton, George	53
Stodard, Thomas	30, 31
Stoke, John de	7
Stokker, Margaret	84, 85, 88
Sir William	84, 85, 88
Stone, Mr. (The King's Surveyor)	55
Stonne, William	78
Stonor, Elizabeth	84
Stow, John	19, 20
Strete, Simond	74
Suffolk, Wratting	9
Surrey, Earl of	35
Surrey, Lambeth	86
Loseley Park	18
Tooting Bec	14, 15, 18
Sutherland, Millicent Duchess of	17
"Swan"—a tenement	87
Syon House	90
Tailor, John	38
Talbot, Dr. William, D.D.	3, 52
Tate, John	14, 85, 91
Tate, otherwise Wood, Margery, wife of Sir Robert Tate	17, 89, 91
Tate, Robert	91
Tate, Sir Robert, Alderman	11, 16, 17, 18, 20, 25, 85, 87, 89, 90, 91
Taylor, Bishop	35, 37
Templars, Knights	6, 7, 8
Thames, galleys on	43
Thele	68
Thomas, John, B.C.L.	53
Thomson, William	29
Thurgood, Henry	46
Thynne, William	36
Tighe, Dr. Robert, S.T.B.	39, 42, 53
Tilling or Tylling, Sir William	31, 33, 34, 72, 75
Tiptoft, John, Earl of Worcester	14, 15
Toc H	51
Tollesbury, Essex	2
Toms, West and	56
Tonge, William de	28
Tooting Bec, Manor of	14, 15, 18

	Page
Tottenham – – – – –	87
Tower Hamlet – – – –	48
Tower Hill– 13, 15, 18, 20, 34, 35, 37, 43, 44	
Tower of London, see London, Tower of	
Tower Street – 4, 16, 18, 36, 40, 44, 45, 47, 48, 49, 58, 86, 87	
Tower Ward – – – – –	44
Tower Watergate – – – –	36
Tremenel, Peter – – – –	6, 9
Trinity Square – – – – –	2, 51
Tun Prison on Cornhill – – –	4
Turke, Godwin – – – –	32
Parnel – – – – –	33
Turkey Company – – – –	45
Twin, Samuel – – – –	47
Tyburn, Manor of – – – –	1
Tyldesley, William – – – –	41
Tyndale, William – – –	35
Tyrwhit, Richard – – – 38, 39, 52	
Underground Railway – – – –	20
Vale, Sir John – – – – 11, 31	
Vessey, Lord de (Vesci) – – –	87
Vestry, Select – – 34, 39, 42, 44, 45, 47, 48, 51, 64, 65	
Vicarage House – – – 45, 46, 56	
Vicarie, Thomas – – – –	19
Vintry Ward – – – 66, 87	
Virby, otherwise Vyrby, Thomas, 12, 13, 23, 24, 33, 52, 74	
Vitull, Walter – – – –	87
Waits of London – – – 25, 90	
Walpole, Sir Horace – – – –	17
Walsingham, Thomas – – – –	13
Walter, Bishop of Rochester – –	1
Walton, William – – – –	23
Warde, W. – – – –	66
Warwick, John Dudley, Earl of – –	18
Warwickshire – – – –	91
Water (formerly Spurier) Lane – –	33
Waterbearer, John the – – –	5
Wat Tyler – – – –	23
Welbeck, William – – – –	78
Welles, William de – – – –	6
Welsh – – – – 11, 67, 68	

	Page
Welton, Dame Margery 22, 23, 24, 26, 74, 75	
West and Toms – – – –	56
Westchepe – – – –	87
Westminster Abbey – – – – 4, 24	
Wharves, see Quays	
Whichelo, C. J. M. – – – –	56
White, Henry – – – –	66
White, Robert – – – –	31
Whitehead, John – – – –	5
Whitgift, John, Archbishop of Canterbury	39
Whittington, Richard, Mayor of London –	10
Wibourne, Widow – – – –	46
Wignall, Roger – – – –	18
William III and Mary – – –	50
Winchester, Bishop of – – –	7
Andrewes, Lancelot – – –	39
Winter, otherwise Wynter, George 19, 20	
Winter, Sir William – – – 19, 20	
Withe, Hugh – – – –	13
Witney, Co. Oxon – – –	4
Wode, Thomas à – – – 30, 56	
Wolde, Robert de la – – – –	6
Wood, Margery, wife of Sir Robert Tate 17, 89, 91	
Wood, Richard, S.T.P. – – 39, 52	
Wood Street – – – –	86
Woodham Walter, Co. Essex –	36
Woodville, Elizabeth, Queen Consort –	14
Wool Wharf – – – –	5
Worcester, Latimer, Hugh, Bishop of 35, 37	
Dr. George Hickes, Dean of –	50
Tiptoft, John, Earl of – – 14, 15	
Wormewell, Walter – – –	46
Worrall, Bartholomew – – –	30
Wratting, Co. Suffolk – – –	9
Wulfghar, King – – – –	1
Wyatt, Sir Thomas – – –	37
Wyche, Richard – – – 12, 13	
Wygeton, Gilbert de – –	52
Wyllaston, John – – –	70
Wyne, John – – – –	52
Wysdale, John – – – –	18
Yelde, John – – – 18, 36	
York, Cecily, Duchess of – – –	14
Richard, Duke of – – –	14
Yorkshire, Hull – – – –	43

Plates, Nos. 1 to 90

PLATE 1

Church of all hallows Barking - Tower Street

EXTERIOR FROM THE
SOUTH-EAST, *c.* 1800

PLATE 2

EXTERIOR FROM THE
SOUTH-EAST, *c.* 1803

PLATE 3

ALLHALLOWS BARKING.

This Church was originally in the gift of the Abbess and Convent of Barking in Essex, whence as a distinction from other Churches in the City of the same dedication, it received its name. We cannot learn when it was founded; but a Vicarage was endowed here some time prior to the Year 1317. In 1649 it was damaged by an explosion of Gunpowder, which destroyed nearly 60 of the adjoining Houses. The Steeple was added in 1659, and having escaped the great Fire was repaired in 1704. The Vicar is the Revd James Johnes M.A.

EXTERIOR FROM THE
SOUTH-EAST, *c.* 1819

PLATE 4

EXTERIOR FROM THE
EAST, *c.* 1837

PLATE 5

EXTERIOR FROM THE EAST
THE SKETCH FOR PLATE 4

PLATE 6

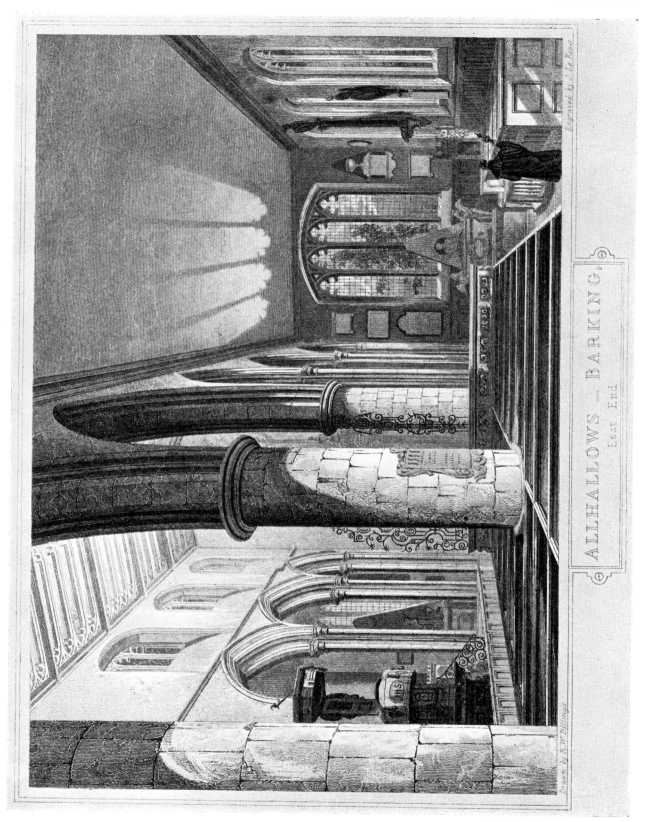

ALLHALLOWS – BARKING.
East End

Drawn by R. W. Billings.   Engraved by J. H. Le Keux.

INTERIOR FROM THE
WEST, c. 1837

PLATE 7

INTERIOR FROM THE WEST
SKETCH FOR PLATE 6

PLATE 8

EXTERIOR FROM THE
NORTH-WEST, 1884

PLATE 9

ALL HALLOWS BARKING, TOWER WARD E.C.

Scale of Feet.

CRYPT BELOW SOUTH CHAPEL

NORTH CHAPEL

NORTH AISLE

NORTH PORCH

UP

VESTRY

CHANCEL

NAVE

SOUTH CHAPEL

FONT

Down

SOUTH AISLE

TOWER

Window above

MODERN WAREHOUSE

GREAT TOWER STREET.

13TH CENTURY.

14TH "

15TH "

17TH & EARLY 18TH

MODERN

UNCERTAIN DATE.

PLATE 10

NORTH E...

Scale ...

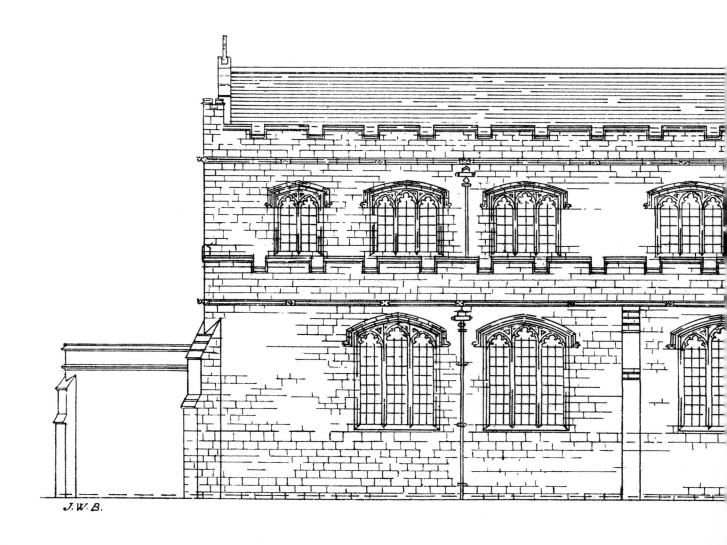

J.W.B.

E

W

20   30

PLATE 11

EXTERIOR FROM THE
NORTH-EAST, *c.* 1910

PLATE 12

EXTERIOR FROM THE
NORTH-WEST, 1928

PLATE 13

TOWER FROM THE
NORTH, *c.* 1910

PLATE 14

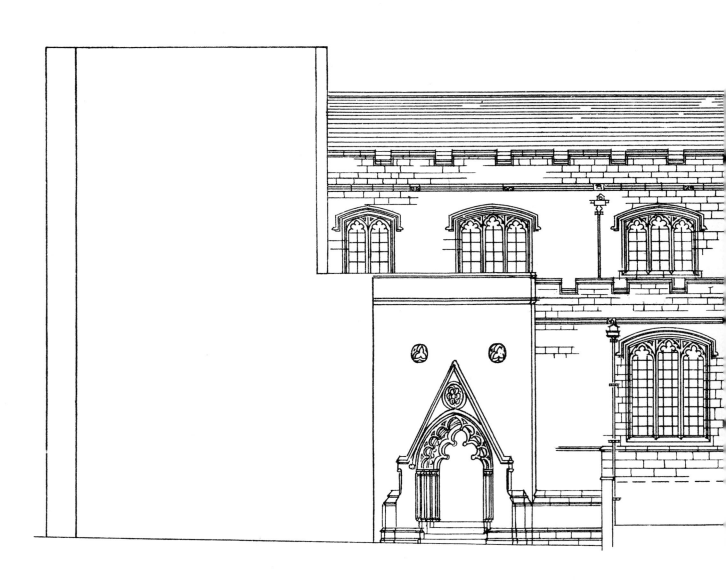

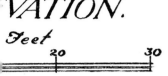

VATION.

Feet

20   30

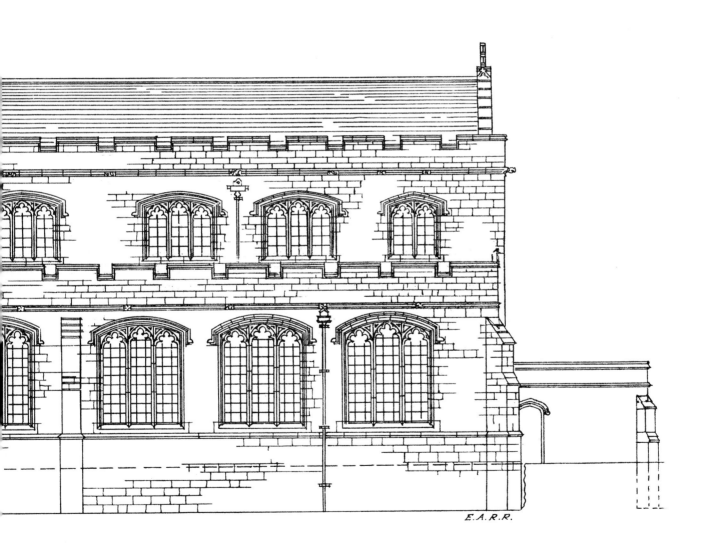

E.A.R.R.

PLATE 15

EXTERIOR FROM THE
SOUTH-EAST, 1926

PLATE 16

SOUTH PORCH AND
TURRET STAIR, *c.* 1863

PLATE 17

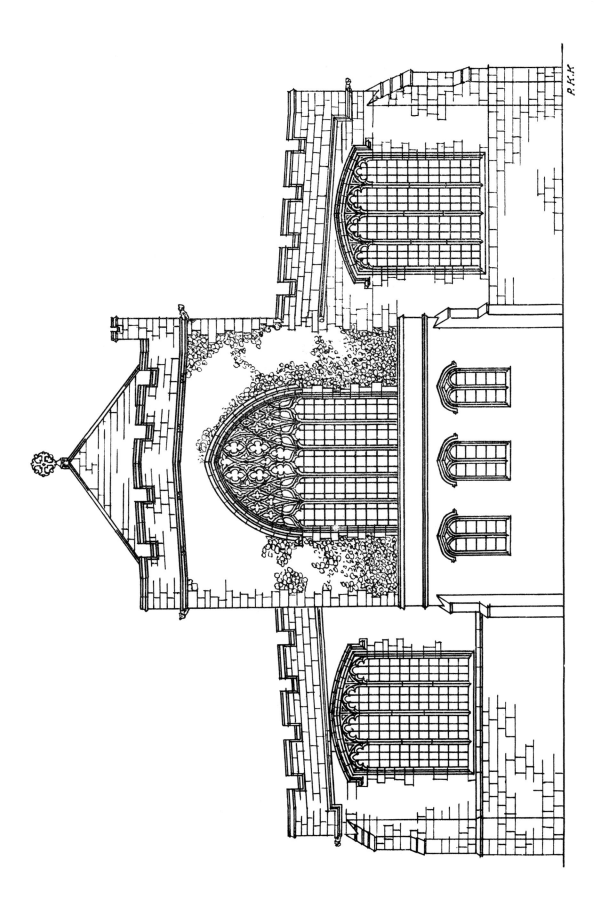

EAST ELEVATION.

Scale of Feet.

PLATE 18

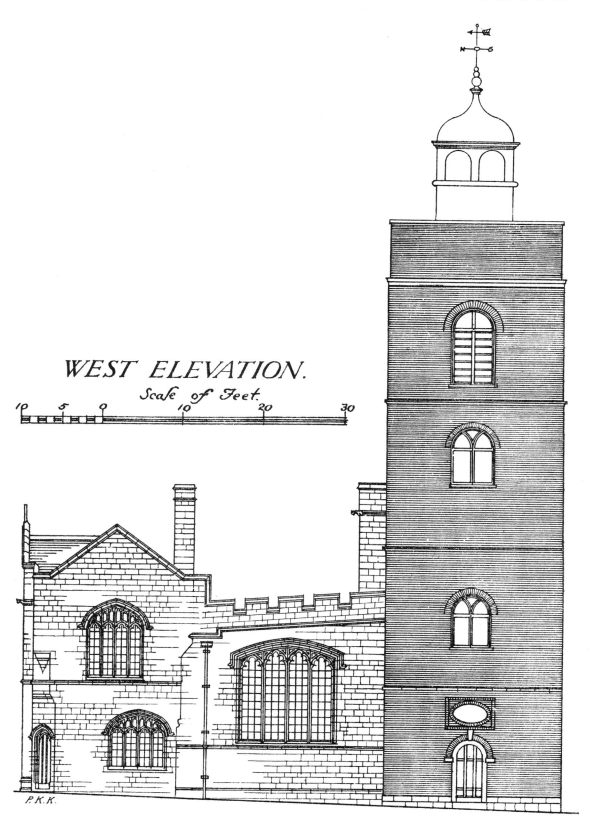

WEST ELEVATION.

Scale of Feet.

P.K.K.

PLATE 19

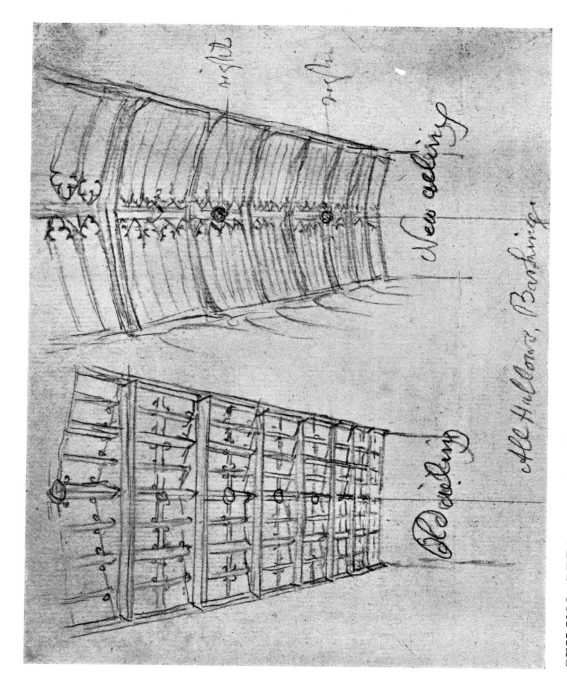

CEILING BEFORE AND AFTER
RECONSTRUCTION IN 1770

PLATE 20

INTERIOR, LOOKING EAST, *c.* 1875
WITH PLASTER CEILING OF 1814
AND HIGH PEWS

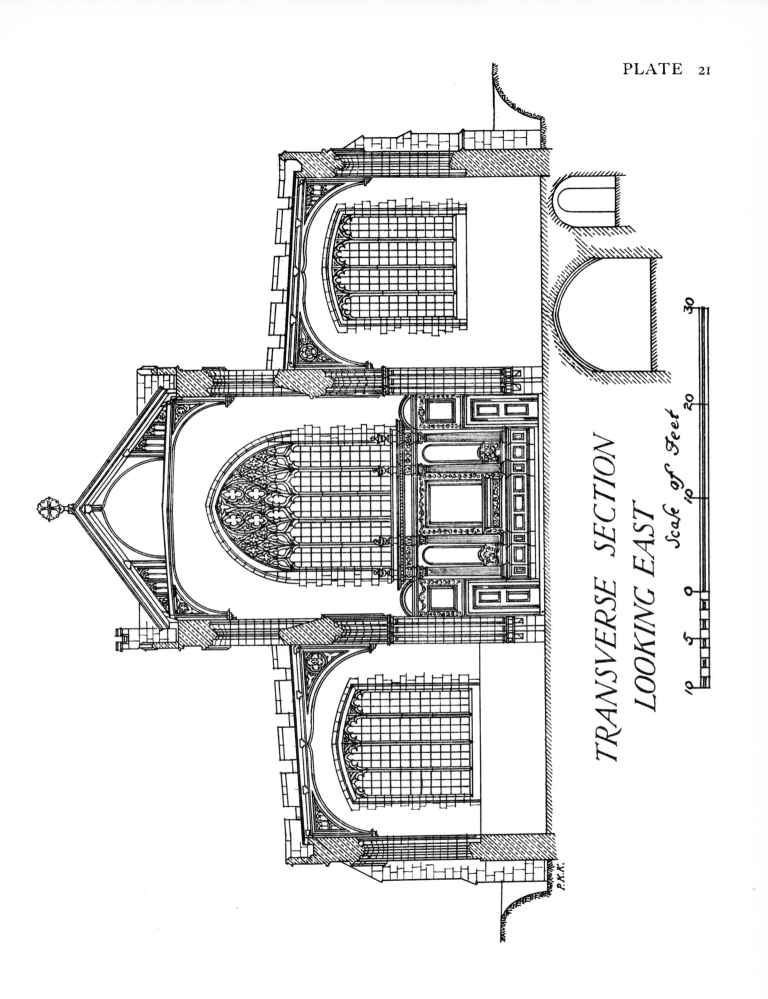

PLATE 21

TRANSVERSE SECTION
LOOKING EAST

Scale of Feet

PLATE 22

INTERIOR, LOOKING EAST, *c.* 1910
WITH MODERN OPEN TIMBER ROOF
AND PEWS CUT DOWN

PLATE 23

INTERIOR, LOOKING EAST, 1926
WITHOUT SCREEN AND SWORD IRONS

PLATE 24

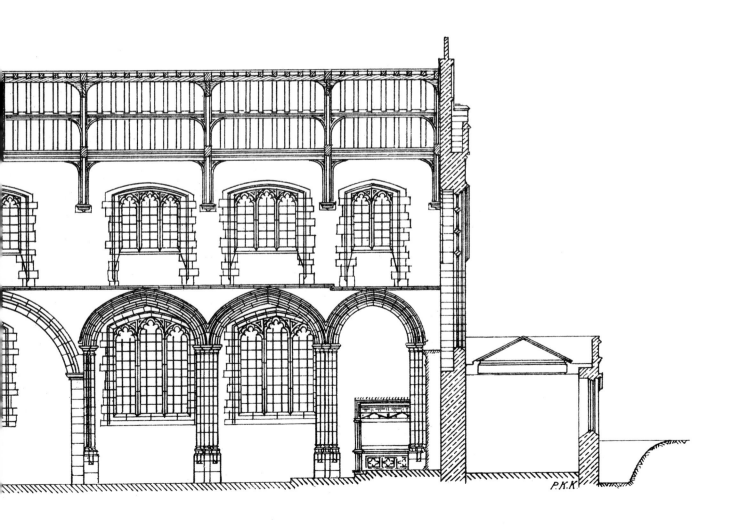

SECTION

Feet

20   30

P.K.K

PLATE 25

NAVE, LOOKING EAST, SHOWING
DETAIL OF NORTH ARCADE, 1927

PLATE 26

NORTH AISLE,
LOOKING EAST, *c.* 1910

PLATE 27

NORTH CHANCEL AISLE,
LOOKING EAST, *c.* 1910

PLATE 28

SOUTH AISLE FROM
NORTH AISLE, *c.* 1910

PLATE 29

EAST END OF THE
CHANCEL ARCADES, *c.* 1910

PLATE 30

CHANCEL AND NAVE ARCADES FROM
THE NORTH-EAST, *c.* 1910

PLATE 31

SOUTH ARCADE, SHOWING
JUNCTION OF STYLES

PLATE 32

BASES TO PIER
AT JUNCTION
OF STYLES

BASES TO PIERS
SOUTH CHANCEL
ARCADE

PLATE 33

SOUTH AISLE, LOOKING
EAST, *c.* 1910

PLATE 34

SOUTH AISLE, LOOKING
WEST, *c.* 1910

PLATE 35

SOUTH CHANCEL
AISLE, *c.* 1910

PLATE 36

THE ORGAN AND THE
CHURCHWARDENS' PEWS,
1927

PLATE 37

CRYPT, LOOKING
WEST, 1927

PLATE 38

CRYPT, LOOKING
EAST, 1928

PLATE 39

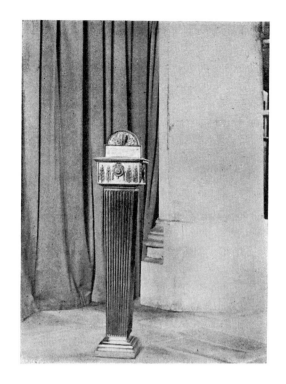

ALMS BOX FROM
CHRIST'S HOSPITAL

POST-RESTORATION
CHAIR

PLATE 40

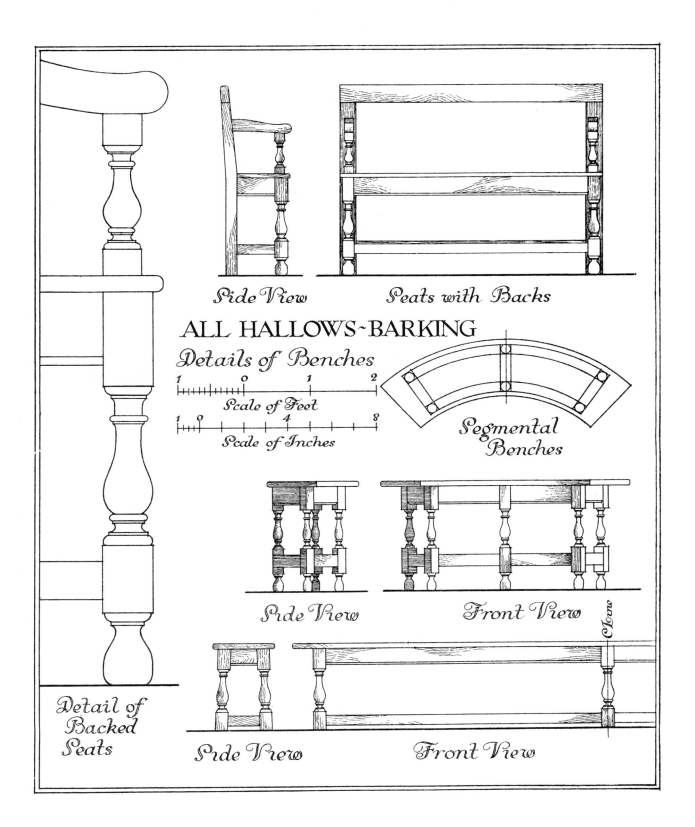

Side View   Seats with Backs

ALL HALLOWS~BARKING

Details of Benches

Scale of Feet

Scale of Inches

Segmental Benches

Side View   Front View

Detail of Backed Seats

Side View   Front View

PLATE 41

CISTERN IN TOWER

PLATE 42

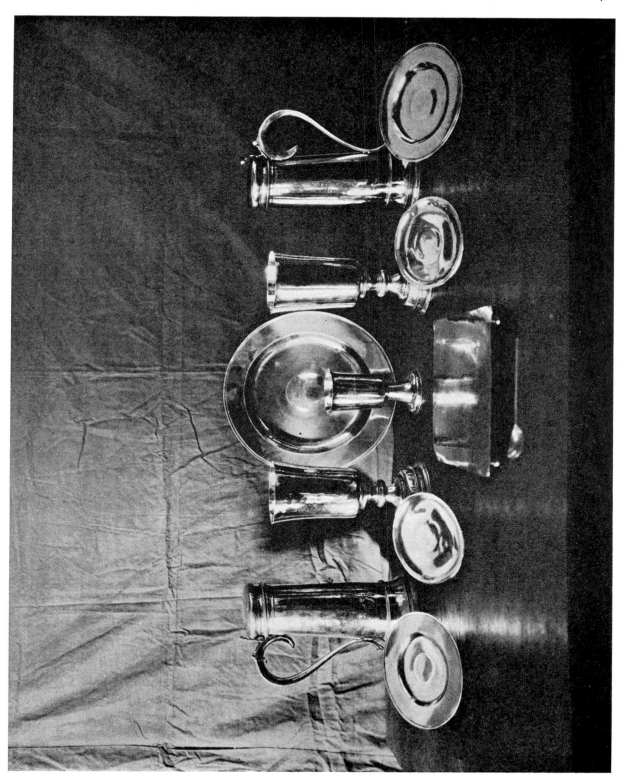

PLATE 43

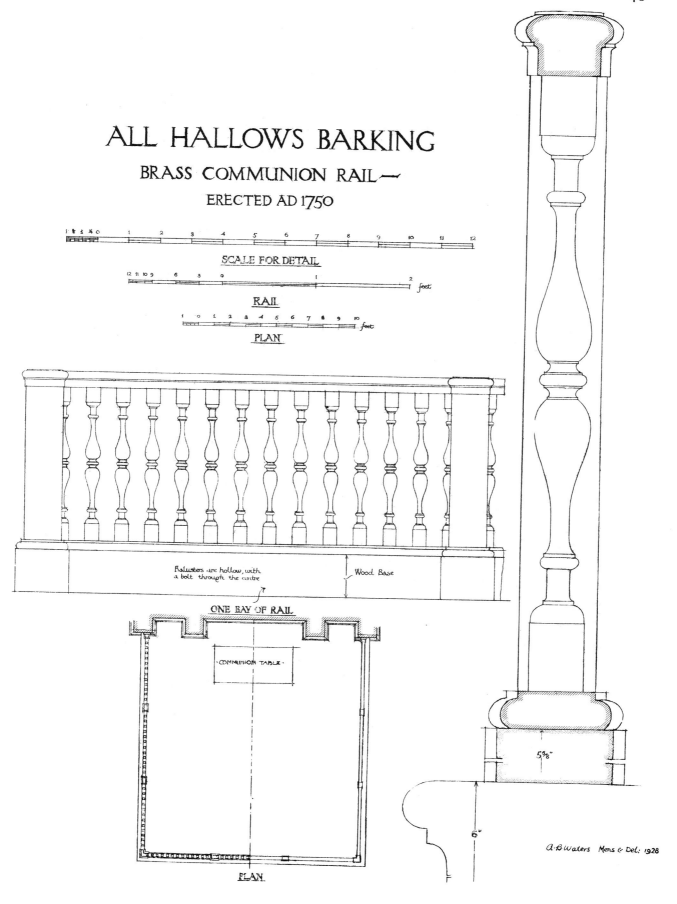

ALL HALLOWS BARKING

BRASS COMMUNION RAIL⁓

ERECTED AD 1750

SCALE FOR DETAIL

RAIL

PLAN

Balusters are hollow, with
a bolt through the centre

Wood Base

ONE BAY OF RAIL

·COMMUNION TABLE·

PLAN

5⅜"

6"

A·B·Waters Mens & Del: 1928

PLATE 44

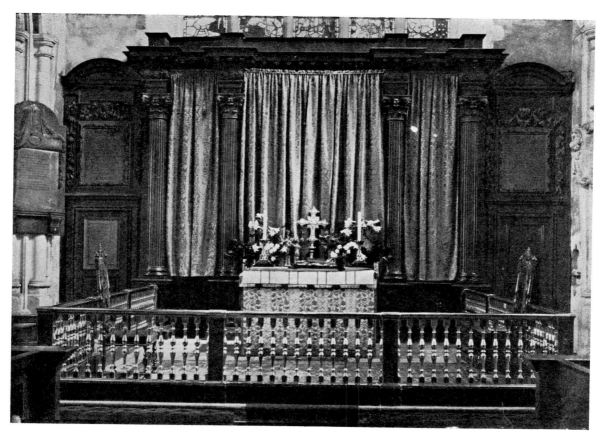

COMMUNION RAILS

PLATE 45

COMMUNION TABLE

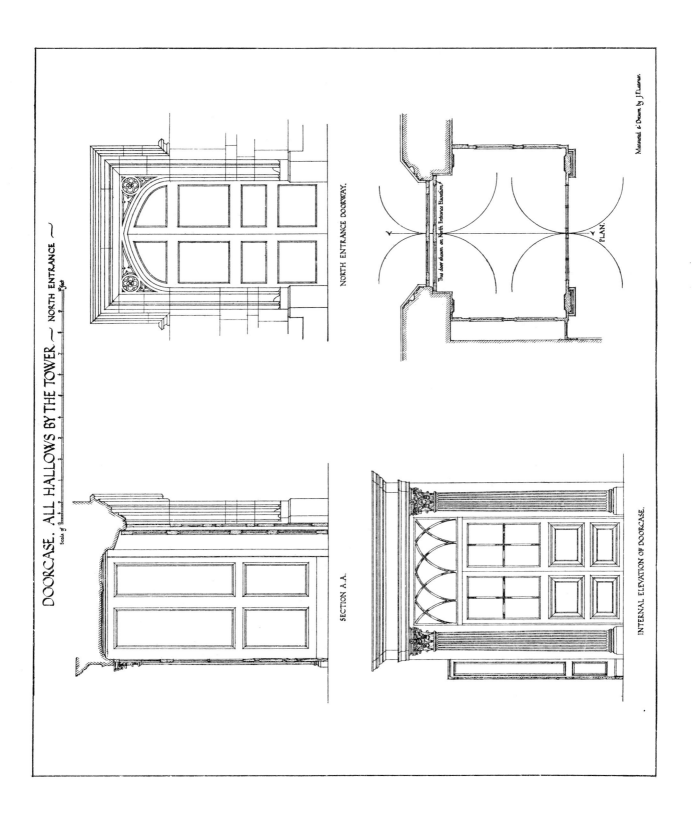

PLATE 46

DOORCASE. ALL HALLOWS BY THE TOWER. ~ NORTH ENTRANCE ~

NORTH ENTRANCE DOORWAY.

PLAN.

Measured & Drawn by J.F.Luxmur.

SECTION A.A.

INTERNAL ELEVATION OF DOORCASE.

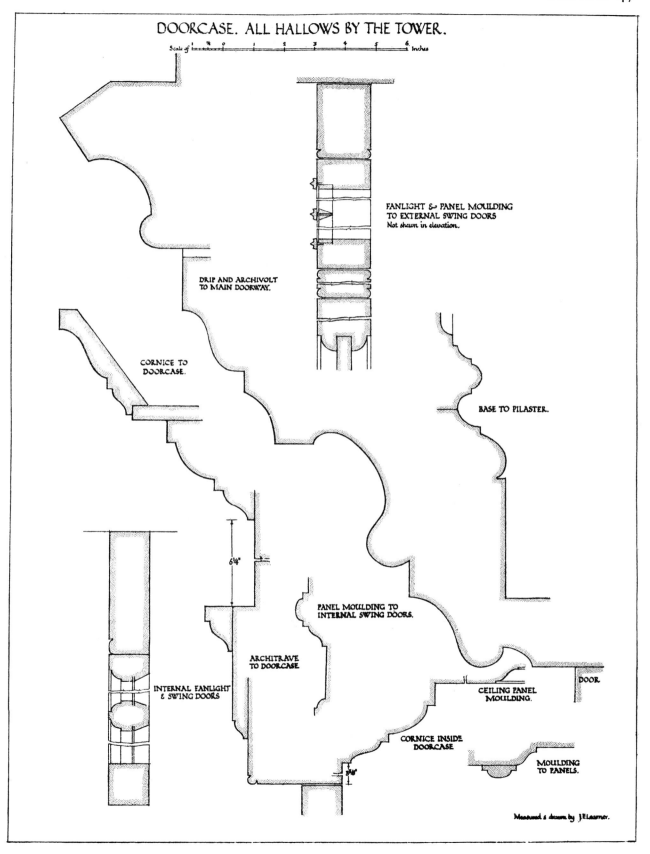

PLATE 47

DOORCASE. ALL HALLOWS BY THE TOWER.

Scale of [............] Inches

FANLIGHT & PANEL MOULDING
TO EXTERNAL SWING DOORS
Not shewn in elevation.

DRIP AND ARCHIVOLT
TO MAIN DOORWAY.

CORNICE TO
DOORCASE.

BASE TO PILASTER.

6¼"

PANEL MOULDING TO
INTERNAL SWING DOORS.

ARCHITRAVE
TO DOORCASE

INTERNAL FANLIGHT
& SWING DOORS

CEILING PANEL
MOULDING.

DOOR

CORNICE INSIDE
DOORCASE

MOULDING
TO PANELS.

Measured & drawn by J.E.Leamer.

PLATE 48

DOORWAY TO
NORTH PORCH

PLATE 49

DOORWAY TO TURRET
STAIRS, SOUTH AISLE

PLATE 50

ALTAR TOMB IN
SOUTH AISLE

PLATE 51

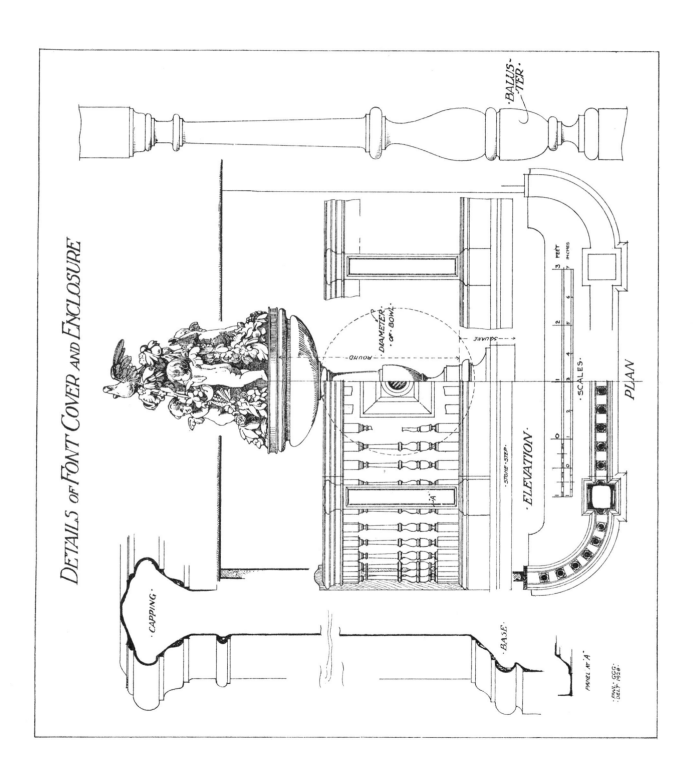

DETAILS of FONT COVER and ENCLOSURE

· BALUS-TER ·

· CAPPING ·

· BASE ·

· ELEVATION ·

· PLAN ·

· SCALES ·

· STONE · STEP ·

· DIAMETER · OF · BOWL ·

· ROUND · · SQUARE ·

· PANEL · N° 'A' ·

· PWL · GCG ·
· DELT · 1928 ·

FEET 3

INCHES

PLATE 52

FONT AND
ENCLOSURE

PLATE 53

FONT AND COVER

PLATE 54

FONT-COVER, LOOKING
TO THE FACE OF DOVE

PLATE 55

FONT-COVER, LOOKING TO
BACK OF DOVE

PLATE 56

17TH-CENTURY GLASS PANEL

PLATE 57

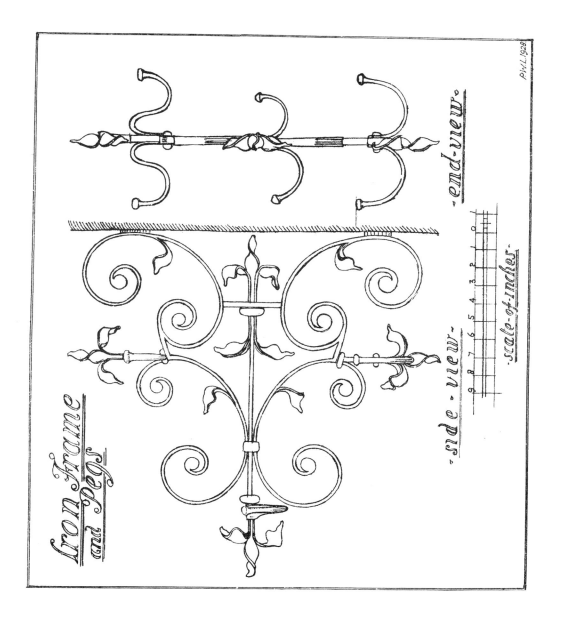

Iron Frame and Pegs

-end-view-

-side-view-

-scale-of-inches-

9 8 7 6 5 4 3 2 1 0

P.W.L.1928

PLATE 58

IRON FRAME
AND PEGS

PLATE 59

THE ORGAN CASE

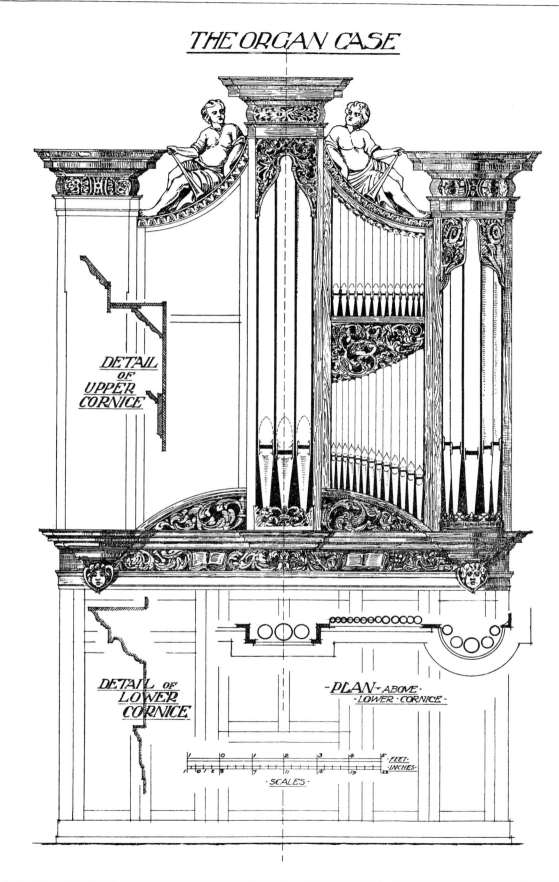

DETAIL
OF
UPPER
CORNICE

DETAIL OF
LOWER
CORNICE

·PLAN· ABOVE
·LOWER·CORNICE·

·SCALES·

PLATE 60

GENERAL VIEW OF ORGAN
AND GALLERY

PLATE 61

DETAIL VIEW OF
ORGAN CASE

PLATE 62

STUART COAT ON
ORGAN GALLERY

PLATE 63

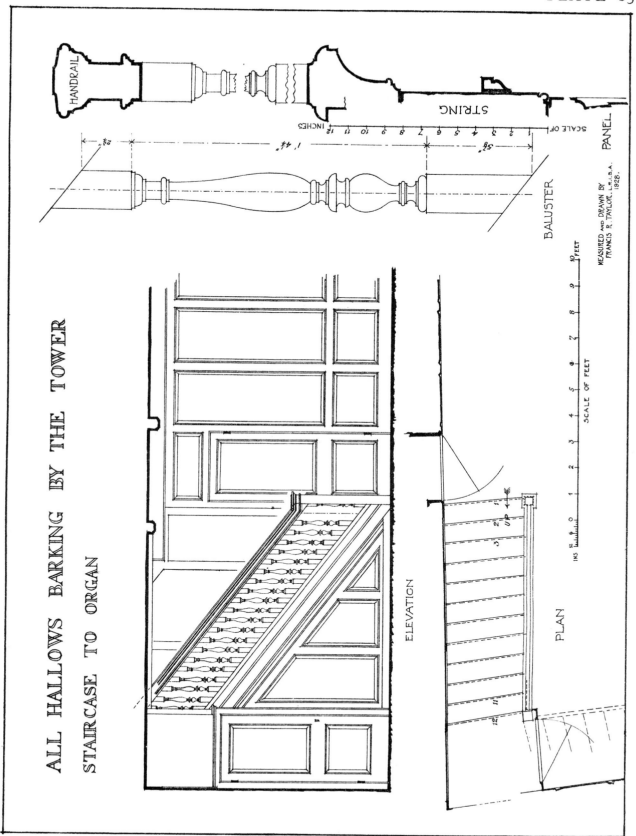

ALL HALLOWS BARKING BY THE TOWER

STAIRCASE TO ORGAN

HANDRAIL

STRING

SCALE OF INCHES

BALUSTER

PANEL

MEASURED AND DRAWN BY
FRANCIS R. TAYLOR, L.R.I.B.A.
1928.

ELEVATION

PLAN

SCALE OF FEET

PLATE 64

DETAIL OF STAIRS UNDER
ORGAN GALLERY

PLATE 65

PISCINA IN
EAST WALL

PLATE 66

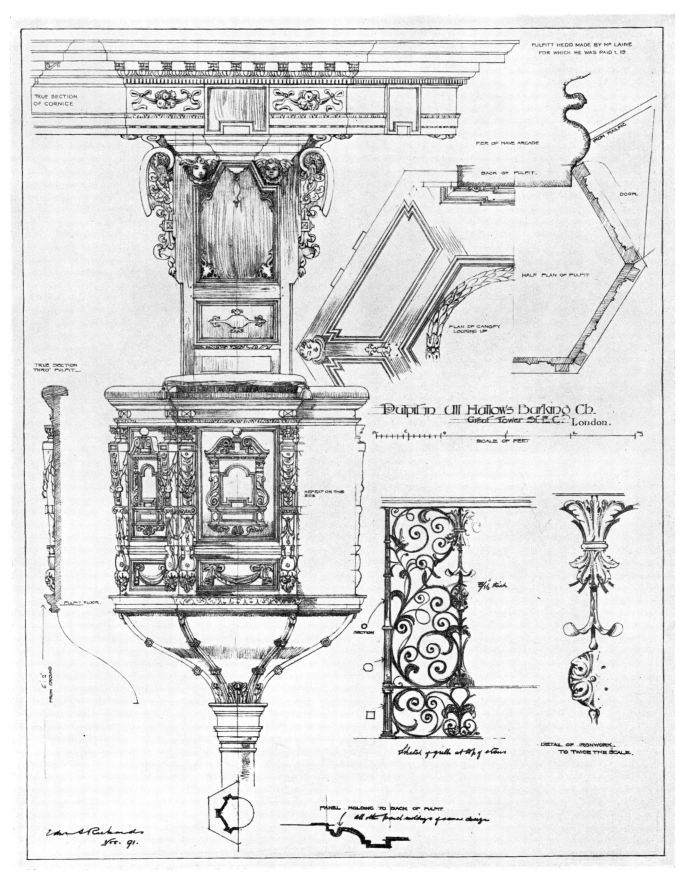

TRUE SECTION
OF CORNICE.

PULPITT HEDD MADE BY Mr LAINE
FOR WHICH HE WAS PAID £. 19

PIER OF NAVE ARCADE

BACK OF PULPIT.

DOOR.

HALF PLAN OF PULPIT

PLAN OF CANOPY
LOOKING UP

TRUE SECTION
THRO' PULPIT

Pulpit in All Hallow's Barking Ch.
Great Tower St. E.C. London.

SCALE OF FEET

REPEAT ON THE
SIDE.

PULPIT FLOOR.

6' 2"
FROM GROUND

SECTION

5/16 thick

Sketch of grille at top of stairs

DETAIL OF IRONWORK.
TO TWICE THE SCALE.

PANEL MOLDING TO BACK OF PULPIT
All other panel moldings of same design

Edward Richards
Nov. 91.

DETAIL OF PULPIT

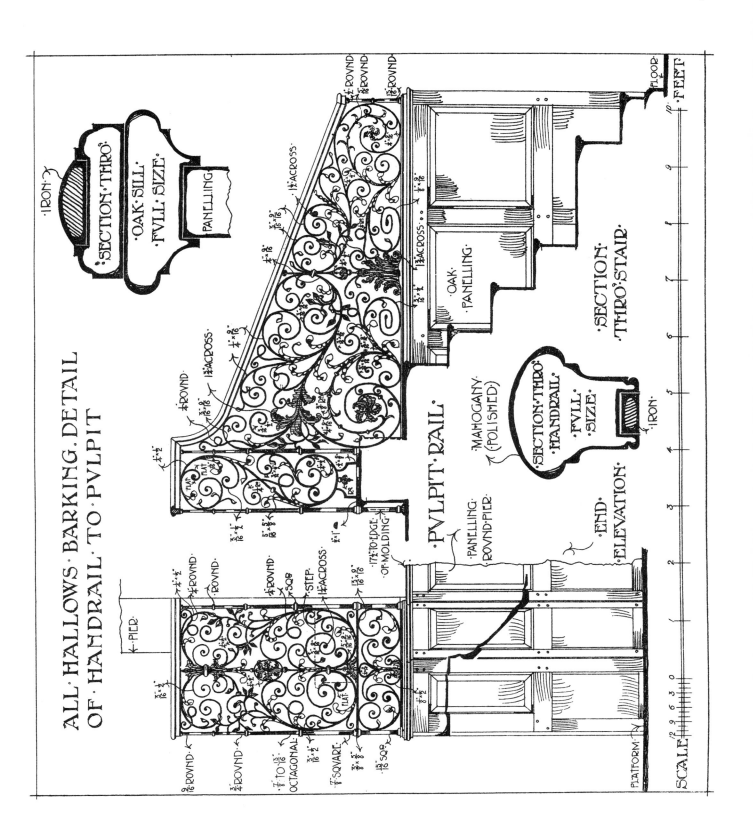

PLATE 67

PLATE 68

PULPIT FROM THE
SOUTH-WEST

PLATE 69

PULPIT, SHOWING HANDRAIL
AND READING-DESK, *c.* 1910

PLATE 70

CARVED PANEL AND CONSOLE
TO PULPIT STAIRS, 1928

PLATE 71

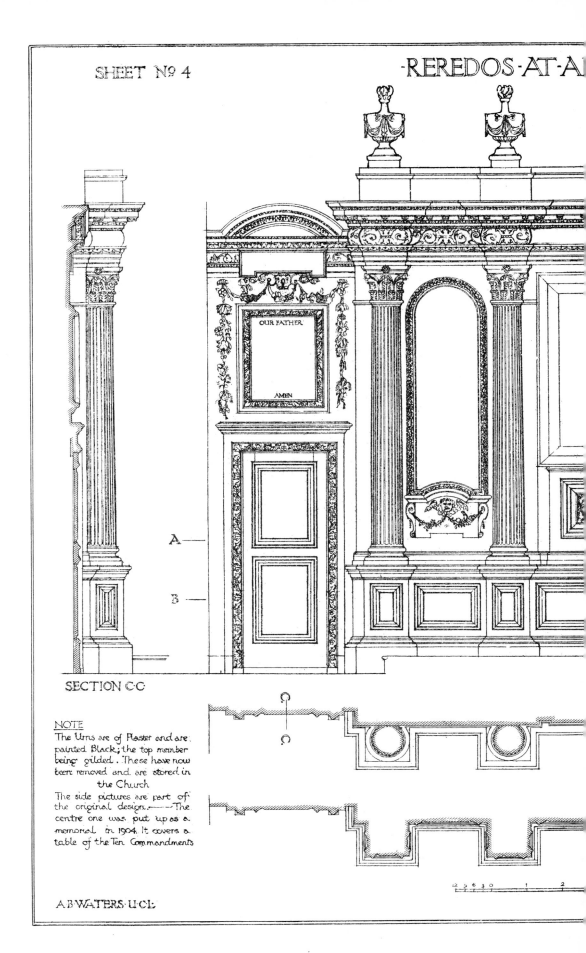

SECTION C·C

<u>NOTE</u>
The Urns are of Plaster and are
painted Black; the top member
being gilded. These have now
been removed and are stored in
the Church
The side pictures are part of
the original design.——The
centre one was put up as a
memorial in 1904. It covers a
table of the Ten Commandments

OUR FATHER

AMEN

A

B

A·B·WATERS·U·C·L·

ALLOWS·BARKING ~

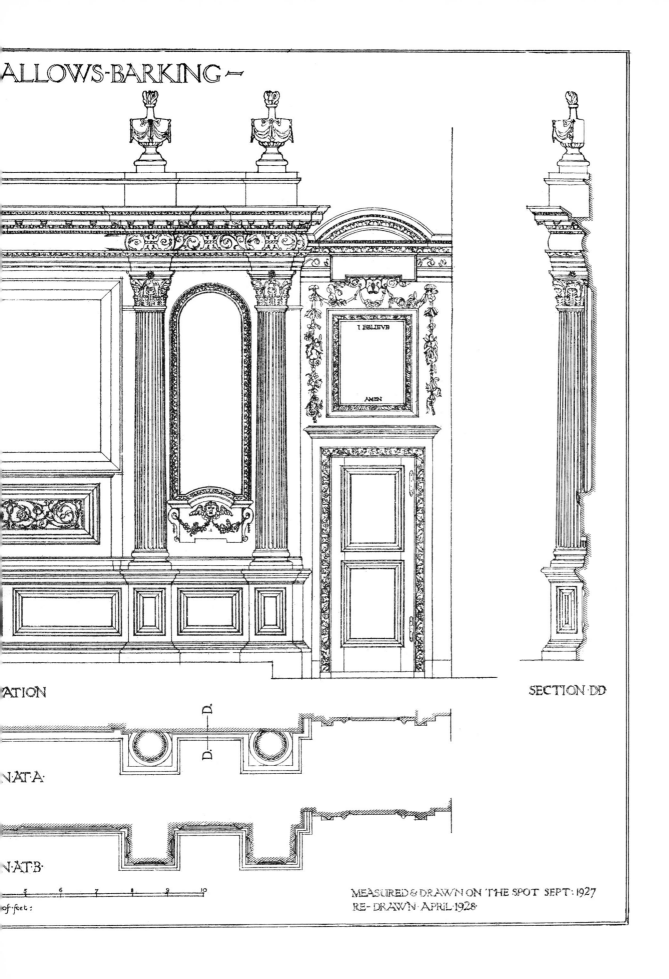

I BELIEVE

AMEN

SECTION·DD

ATION

D.

D.

N·AT·A·

N·AT·B·

5   6   7   8   9   10

of·feet :

MEASURED & DRAWN ON THE SPOT SEPT: 1927
RE-DRAWN·APRIL·1928·

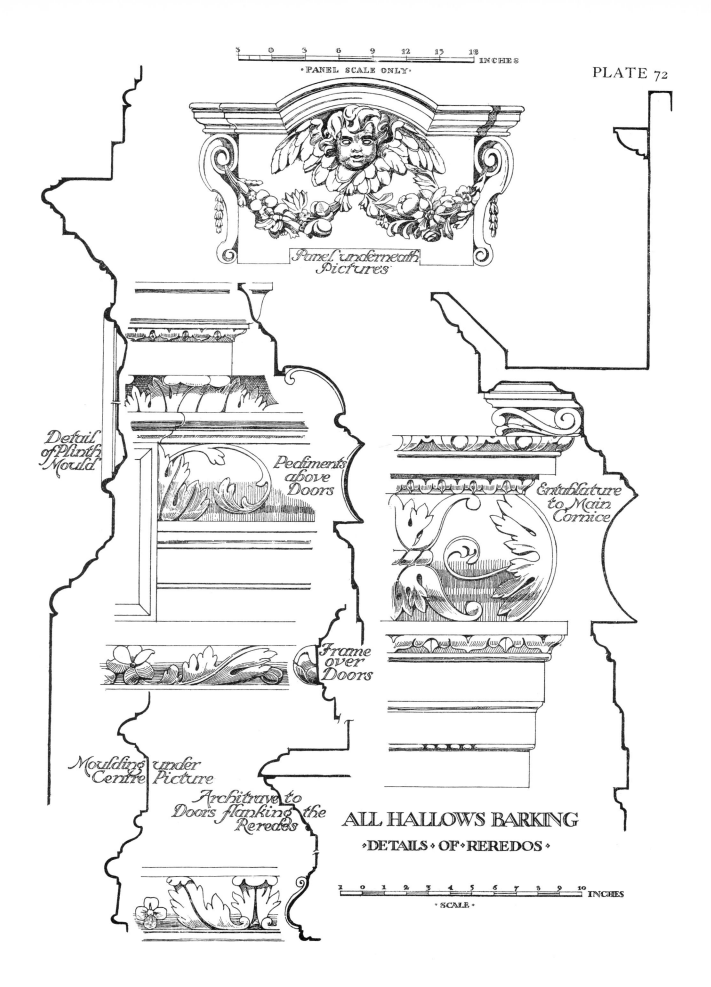

PLATE 72

5 0 3 6 9 12 15 18 INCHES
·PANEL SCALE ONLY·

Panel underneath Pictures

Detail of Plinth Mould

Pediments above Doors

Entablature to Main Cornice

Frame over Doors

Moulding under Centre Picture

Architrave to Doors flanking the Reredos

ALL HALLOWS BARKING
·DETAILS·OF·REREDOS·

1 0 1 2 3 4 5 6 7 8 9 10 INCHES
·SCALE·

PLATE 73

REREDOS, NORTH SIDE

PLATE 74

REREDOS, SOUTH SIDE

PLATE 75

CONSOLE PANELS IN REREDOS

PLATE 76

DETAIL OF SCREENS

PLATE 77

DETAILS OF PANELLING ENCLOSING
PEWS, W. END OF NAVE.

SCALE OF FEET

12 INS
0
1
2

P.K.K.
Mens et Delt

PLATE 78

Pierced Panel in Pew Front.

*Carved Panels in Screen
at back of Pews.*

*P.K.K.
M. st D*

PLATE 79

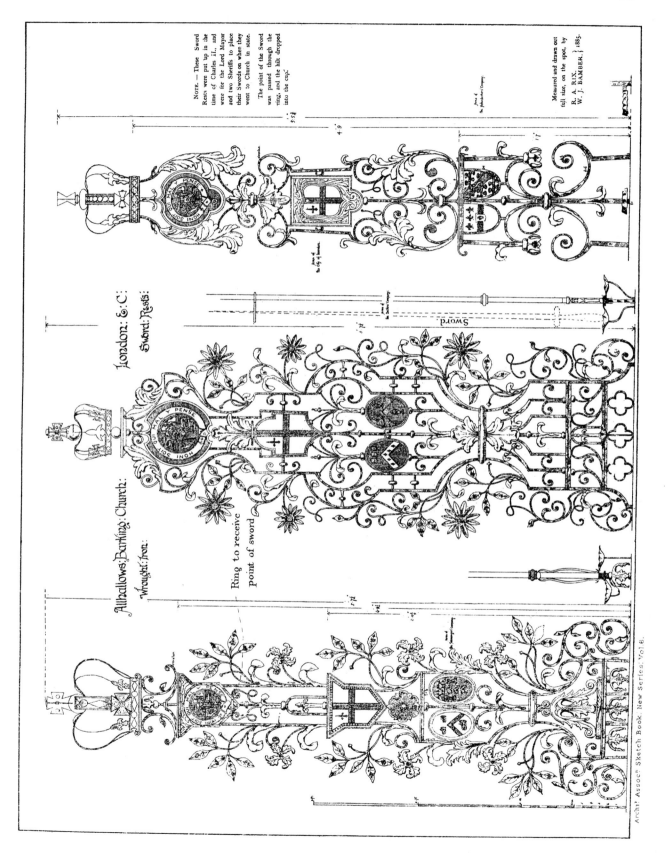

London: E.C:
Sword: Rests:

Allhallows: Barking: Church:

Wrought: Iron:

Ring to receive
point of sword

Sword

NOTE. — These Sword Rests were put up in the time of Charles II, and were for the Lord Mayor and two Swords to place their Swords on when they went to Church in state.

The point of the Sword was passed through the ring, and the hilt dropped into the cup.

Measured and drawn out full size, on the spot, by R. A. RIX. W. J. BAMBER. } 1885.

PLATE 80

THE SWORD-RESTS, 1928

PLATE 81

SWORD-REST, SIR
JOHN EYLES

PLATE 82

SWORD-REST,
SLINGSBY BETHELL

PLATE 83

SWORD-REST, SIR
THOMAS CHITTY

PLATE 84

WEST WINDOW,
NORTH AISLE

PLATE 85

SAINT MATTHEW

SAINT MARK

PANELS IN CHURCHWARDENS' SEATS

PLATE 86

SAINT LUKE

SAINT JOHN

PANELS IN CHURCHWARDENS' SEATS

PLATE 87

PANELS IN CHURCH-
WARDENS' SEATS

PLATE 88

PANELS IN CHURCH-
WARDENS' SEATS

PLATE 89

PANELS IN CHURCH-
WARDENS' SEATS

PLATE 90

PANELS IN CHURCH-
WARDENS' SEATS